To the Reader

This Book Belongs To

_____

SCIENTOLOGY
A NEW SLANT ON
Life

SCIENTOLOGY
A NEW SLANT ON
Life

L. RON HUBBARD

Bridge
Publications, Inc.

A
HUBBARD®
PUBLICATION

BRIDGE PUBLICATIONS, INC.
4751 Fountain Avenue
Los Angeles, California 90029

ISBN 978-1-4031-4488-1

Important Note

In reading this book, be very certain you never go past a word you do not fully understand. The only reason a person gives up a study or becomes confused or unable to learn is because he or she has gone past a word that was not understood.

The confusion or inability to grasp or learn comes AFTER a word the person did not have defined and understood. It may not only be the new and unusual words you have to look up. Some commonly used words can often be misdefined and so cause confusion.

This datum about not going past an undefined word is the most important fact in the whole subject of study. Every subject you have taken up and abandoned had its words which you failed to get defined.

Therefore, in studying this book be very, very certain you never go past a word you do not fully understand. If the material becomes confusing or you can't seem to grasp it, there will be a word just earlier that you have not understood. Don't go any further, but go back to BEFORE you got into trouble, find the misunderstood word and get it defined.

Glossary

To aid reader comprehension, L. Ron Hubbard directed the editors to provide a glossary. This is included in the Appendix, *Editor's Glossary of Words, Terms and Phrases*. Words sometimes have several meanings. The *Editor's Glossary* only contains the definitions of words as they are used in this text. Other definitions can be found in standard language or Dianetics and Scientology dictionaries.

If you find any other words you do not know, look them up in a good dictionary.

Contents

INTRODUCTION

SCIENTOLOGY:
A NEW SLANT ON LIFE

L. RON HUBBARD

INTRODUCTION

WHO ARE YOU ANYWAY? Where do you come from? What will happen to you? Are you a product of the mud as you have been told, to exist for a few years and then wither away and fertilize the earth from which they said you came? Or are you something better, something finer?

What are your goals? Where are you going? Why are you here? What *are* you? Scientology has answers to these questions, good answers that are true, answers that work for you. For the subject matter of Scientology is *you*.

L. RON HUBBARD

Is It Possible to Be Happy?

SCIENTOLOGY:
A NEW SLANT ON LIFE

L. RON HUBBARD

" *The truth of the matter*
is that all the happiness
you will ever find
lies in you. "

Is It Possible to Be Happy?

 Is it possible to be happy?

A great many people wonder whether or not happiness even exists in this modern, rushing world. Very often an individual can have a million dollars, he can have everything his heart apparently desires and is still unhappy. We take the case of somebody who has worked all his life. He's worked hard. He's raised a big family. He's looked forward to that time of his life when he, at last, could retire and be happy and be cheerful and have lots of time to do all the things he wanted to do. And then we see him after he's retired and is he happy? No. He's sitting there thinking about the good old days when he was working hard.

Our main problem in life is happiness.

The world today may or may not be designed to be a happy world. It may or may not be possible for you to be happy in this world. And yet, nearly all of us have the goal of being happy and cheerful about existence.

And then, very often, we look around at the world around us and say, "Well, nobody could be happy in this place." We look at the dirty dishes in the sink and the car needing a coat of paint and the fact that we need a new gas heater, we need a new coat, we need new shoes or we'd just like to have better shoes, and say, "Well, how could anybody *possibly* be happy when, actually, he can't have everything he wants? He's unable to do all the things he'd like to do and, therefore, this environment doesn't *permit* a person to be as happy as he could be."

Well, I'll tell you a funny thing. A lot of philosophers have said this many, many times, but the truth of the matter is that all the happiness you will ever find lies in *you*.

You remember when you were maybe five years old and you went out in the morning and you looked at the day–and it was a very, very beautiful day. You looked at flowers and they were *very* beautiful flowers. Twenty-five years later, you get up in the morning, you take a look at the flowers–they are wilted. The day *isn't* a happy day. Well, what's changed? You know they are the same flowers, it's the same world. Something must have changed. Well, probably it was *you*.

Actually, a little child derives all of his pleasure in life from the grace he puts upon life. He waves a magic hand and turns all manner of interesting things into being out in the society. Where does he do this? He goes down and he looks at the cop. Here's this big, strong brute of a man riding this iron steed, up and down. Boy, he'd like to be a cop. Yes sir, he'd sure like to be a cop! Twenty-five years later, he looks at that cop riding up and down, checking his speedometer and says, "Doggone these cops!"

Well, what's changed here? Has the cop changed? No. Just the *attitude* toward the cop. One's attitude toward life makes every possible difference in one's living. You know, you don't have to study a thousand ancient books to discover that fact. But sometimes it needs to be pointed out again that life doesn't change so much as *you*.

Once upon a time, perhaps, you were thinking of being married and having a nice home and having a nice family and everything would be just right. And the husband would come home, you see, and you'd put dinner on the table and everybody would be happy about the whole thing. And then you got married and it maybe didn't quite work out. Somehow or other, he comes home late, he's had an argument with the boss and he doesn't feel well. He doesn't want to go to the movies and he doesn't see how you have any work to do anyhow. After all, you just sit home all day and do nothing. And you know he doesn't do any work either. He disappears out of the house, he's gone and he comes back later in the evening and he hasn't done anything either. Quite an argument could ensue over this and, actually, both of you have worked quite hard.

Well, what do we do in a condition like this? Do we just break up the marriage? Or touch a match to the whole house? Or throw the kids in the garbage can and go home to Mama? Or what do we do?

Well, there are many, many, many things we could do and the least of them is to take a look at the environment. Just look around and say, "Where am I? What *am* I doing *here*?" And then, once you've found out where you were, why, try to find out how you could make that a little more habitable.

The day when you stop building your own environment, when you stop building your own surroundings, when you stop waving a magic hand and gracing everything around you with magic and beauty, things cease to be magical, things cease to be beautiful.

Well, maybe you've just neglected somewhere back in the last few years to wave that magic hand.

Other people seek happiness in various ways. They seek it hectically. It's as though it is some sort of a mechanism that exists. It's made up. Maybe it's a little machine, maybe it's something that's parked in a cupboard or maybe happiness is down at the next corner. Maybe it's someplace else. They are looking for *something*. Well, the odd part of it is, the only time they'll ever find something is when they put it there *first*. Now, this doesn't seem very creditable, but it is quite true.

Those people who have become unhappy about life *are* unhappy about life solely and completely because life has ceased to be made by them. Here we have the single difference in a human being. We have that human being who is unhappy, miserable and isn't getting along in life, who is sick, who doesn't see brightness. Life is handling, running, changing, making *him*. Here we have somebody who is happy, who is cheerful, who is strong, who finds there is something worth doing in life. What do we discover in this person? We find out that he is making life. Now, there is actually the single difference: Are you making life or is life making you?

And when we go into this, we find out that a person has stopped making life because he himself has decided that life cannot be made. Some failure, some small failure–maybe not graduating with the same class, maybe that failure that had to do with not marrying quite the first man or woman who came along and seemed desirable, maybe the failure of having lost a car or just some minor thing in life started this attitude. A person looked around one day and said, "Well, I've lost." And after that, life makes him, he doesn't make life anymore.

Well, this would be a very dreadful situation if nothing could be done about it. But the fact of the matter is it's the easiest problem of all the problems Man faces: changing himself and changing the attitudes of those around him. It's very, very easy to change somebody else's attitude. Yet you are totally dependent upon other people's attitudes. Somebody's attitude toward you may make or break your life. Did it ever occur to you that your home holds together probably because of the attitude the other person has toward you? So there's two problems here. You have to change two attitudes: one, your attitude toward somebody else and, two, their attitude toward you.

Well, are there ways to do these things? Yes, fortunately, there are.

For many, many, many centuries, Man has desired to know how to change the mind and condition of himself and his fellows. Actually, Man hadn't accumulated enough information to do this up to relatively few years ago. But we're living in a very fast-paced world. We're living in a world where magic is liable to occur at any time, and has.

Man now understands a great many things about the universe he lives in which he never understood before. And amongst the things which he now understands is the human mind. The human mind is not an unsolved problem. Nineteenth-century psychology did not solve the problem. That doesn't mean that it hasn't been solved.

In modern times, the most interesting miracles are taking place all across this country and across the other continents of Earth. What do these miracles consist of? They consist of people becoming well. It consists of people who were unhappy becoming happy once more. It consists of abolishing the danger inherent in many of the illnesses and in many of the conditions of Man.

And yet the answer has been with Man all the time. Man has been able to reach out and find this answer, but perhaps Man himself had to change. Perhaps he had to come up into modern times to find out that the physical universe was not composed of demons and ghosts, to outlive his superstitions, to outlive the ignorance of his forebears. Perhaps he had to do everything, including invent the atom bomb, before he could find himself.

Well, he has pretty well mastered the physical universe now. The physical universe is to him, now, rather a pawn–he can do many things with it. And, having conquered that, he can now conquer himself. The truth of the matter is he *has* conquered himself.

Scientology came about because of Man's increased knowledge of energy. Man became possessed of more information about energy than he had ever had before in all of his history. And amongst that, he came into possession of information about the energy which is his own mind.

The body *is* an energy mechanism. Naturally, a person who cannot handle energy could not handle a body. He would be tired, he would be upset, he would be unhappy. As he looks all around him, he finds nothing *but* energy.

If he knew a great deal about energy–particularly the energy of himself, the energy that made him think, the energy that *was* himself and the space which surrounded him–he, of course, would know himself. And that, in the final essence, has been his goal for many thousands of years: to know himself.

Scientology has made it possible for him to do so.

L. Ron Hubbard

Scientology:
An Overview

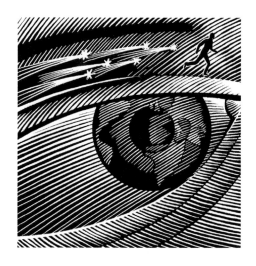

PERSONAL INTEGRITY

SCIENTOLOGY:
A NEW SLANT ON LIFE

L. RON HUBBARD

" What is true

for you is what you

have observed yourself.

And when you lose that,

you have lost everything. "

PERSONAL
INTEGRITY

WHAT IS TRUE FOR YOU is what you have observed *yourself*. And when you lose that, you have lost everything.

What is personal integrity? Personal integrity is *knowing what you know*. What you know is what you know and to have the courage to know and say what you have observed. And that is integrity and there is no other integrity.

Of course, we can talk about honor, truth, nobility–all these things as esoteric terms. But I think they would all be covered very well if what we really observed was what we observed, that we took care to observe what we were observing, that we always *observed* to *observe*. And not necessarily maintaining a skeptical attitude, a critical attitude or an open mind–not necessarily maintaining these things at all–but *certainly* maintaining *sufficient* personal integrity and *sufficient* personal belief and confidence in self and courage that we can observe what we observe and say what we have observed.

Nothing in Scientology is true for you unless you have observed it and it is true according to your observation.

That is all.

A DESCRIPTION OF SCIENTOLOGY

SCIENTOLOGY:
A NEW SLANT ON LIFE

L. RON HUBBARD

" The only truly therapeutic agent in this universe is the spirit. In Scientology this has been demonstrated with more thoroughness and exists with more certainty than the physical sciences or mathematics. "

A DESCRIPTION OF SCIENTOLOGY

SCIENTOLOGY IS THE SCIENCE of knowing how to know answers. It is an organized system of axioms and processes which resolve the problems of existence.

A Scientologist is a specialist in spiritual and human affairs.

Scientology is organized from the viewpoint of the spirit and contains a precise and usable definition of the spirit, and charts and studies and is capable of changing the behavior of the spirit.

Scientology is formed in the tradition of ten thousand years of religious philosophy and considers itself a culmination of the searches which began with the Veda, the Tao, Buddhism, Christianity and other religions. Scientology is a gnostic faith in that it knows it knows. This is its distinguishing characteristic from most of its predecessors. Scientology can demonstrate that it can attain the goals set for Man by all religions, which are wisdom, good health and immortality.

By spiritual means, but means which are as precise as mathematics, a host of the bad conditions of life may be remedied in Scientology.

Illness and malfunction can be divided into two general classes. First, those resulting from the operation of the spirit directly upon the communication networks of life or the body, and those occasioned by the disruption of structure through purely physical causes. Unhappiness, inability to heal and psychosomatic illness (which include some 70 percent of the illnesses of Man) are best healed by immediate address of the human spirit. Illness caused by recognizable bacteria and injury in accident are best treated by physical means and these fall distinctly into the field of medicine and are not the province of Scientology, except that accidents and illness and bacterial infection are predetermined in almost all cases by spiritual malfunction and unrest, and conditions in accidents are definitely prolonged by any spiritual malfunction. Thus we have the field of medicine addressing the immediate injury (such surgical matters as birth and acute infection, and such things as contusions and abrasions resulting from accidents) as well as the administration of drugs and antibiotics to prevent the demise of the patient in a crisis. This is the role of medicine.

Where predisposition to disease or injury exists, or where disease or injury is being prolonged, or where unhappiness and worry causes mental or physical upset, or where we desire to better and improve communications or social relationships, we are dealing, if we are efficient, in the realm of Scientology. For such things are best healed or best prevented or best remedied by immediate and direct recourse to the spirit and its action and determinism of the course of the body.

The only truly therapeutic agent in this universe is the spirit. In Scientology this has been demonstrated with more thoroughness and exists with more certainty than the physical sciences or mathematics. A Scientologist *can* make an individual well, happy and grant him personal immortality, simply by addressing the human spirit.

For more than ten thousand years, Man has been accumulating material toward this goal. But it required a wide understanding of the philosophies and processes of Asia and a thorough indoctrination in the Western physical sciences and mathematics to bring about the precision existing in Scientology when practiced properly by a trained Scientologist. It could be said with Scientology that we have entered the Second Age of Miracles.

It is a discovery of Scientology—a discovery susceptible to the most arduous scientific proofs—that people are not bodies, but that people are living units operating bodies. The living unit we call, in Scientology, a thetan, that being taken from the Greek letter *theta,* the mathematical symbol used in Scientology to indicate the source of life and life itself. The individual, the person, the actual identity, is this living unit. It is modified by the addition of a body. And by the addition of a body, it is brought into a certain unknowingness about its own condition. The mission of Scientology is to raise the knowingness of this spirit to such a degree that it again knows what it is and what it is doing. And in this state the thetan can apply directly to his own body or to his environment or to the bodies of others the healing skill of which he is capable. It is the thetan which builds and constructs, it is the thetan which forms actual forms and organisms.

Among the capabilities and potentials of the thetan is immortality in full knowingness of his own identity. The amount of time which he has spent on Earth and the number of deaths through which he has gone have brought him into a state of forgetfulness about who and where he has been. This material is recovered in Scientology, if the Scientologist specifically processes toward it.

How to
Study Scientology

SCIENTOLOGY:
A NEW SLANT ON LIFE

L. RON HUBBARD

" Do not make the mistake of criticizing something on the basis of whether or not it concurs with the opinions of someone else. The point which is pertinent is whether or not it concurs with your opinion. Does it agree with what you think? "

HOW TO
STUDY SCIENTOLOGY

T HE FIRST THING that a student has to find out for himself, and then recognize, is that he is dealing with precision tools. It isn't up to someone else to force this piece of information on him. The whole subject of Scientology, as far as the student is concerned, is as good or bad in direct ratio to his knowledge of it. It is up to a student to find out how precise these tools are. He should, before he starts to discuss, criticize or attempt to improve on the data presented to him, find out for himself whether or not the mechanics of Scientology are as stated and whether or not it does what has been proposed for it.

He should make up his mind about each thing that is taught–the procedure, techniques, mechanics and theory. He should ask himself these questions: Does this piece of data exist? Is it true? Does it work? Will it produce the best possible results in the shortest time?

There is a way to answer these questions to his own satisfaction: find them himself. These are fundamentals and every student should undertake to discover them himself, thus raising Scientology above an authoritarian category. It is not sufficient that an instructor stand before him and declare the existence of these. Each and every student must determine for himself whether or not the instructor's statements are true.

There are two ways men ordinarily accept things, neither of them very good: One is to accept a statement because Authority says it is true and must be accepted. And the other is by preponderance of agreement amongst other people.

Preponderance of agreement is all too often the general public test for sanity or insanity. Suppose someone were to walk into a crowded room and suddenly point to the ceiling saying, "Oh, look! There's a huge, twelve-foot spider on the ceiling!" Everyone would look up, but no one else would see the spider. Finally, someone would tell him so. "Oh, yes there is," he would declare and become very angry when he found that no one would agree with him. If he continued to declare his belief in the existence of the spider, he would very soon find himself institutionalized.

The basic definition of *sanity* in this somewhat nebulously learned society is whether or not a person agrees with everyone else. It is a very sloppy manner of accepting evidence, but all too often it is the primary measuring stick.

And then the Rule of Authority: "Does Dr. J. Doe agree with your proposition? No? Then, of course, it cannot be true. Dr. Doe is an eminent authority in the field."

A man by the name of Galen at one time dominated the field of medicine. Another man by the name of Harvey upset Galen's cozy position with a new theory of blood circulation. Galen had been agreeing with the people of his day concerning the "tides" of the blood. They knew nothing about heart action. They accepted everything they had been taught and did little observing of their own. Harvey worked at the Royal Medical Academy and found by animal vivisection the actual function of the heart. He had the good sense to keep his findings absolutely quiet for a while. Leonardo da Vinci had somehow discovered or postulated the same thing, but he was a "crazy artist" and no one would believe an artist. Harvey was a member of the audience of a play by Shakespeare in which the playwright made the same observation, but again the feeling that artists never contribute anything to society blocked anyone but Harvey from considering the statement as anything more than fiction.

Finally, Harvey made his announcement. Immediately, dead cats, rotten fruit and pieces of wine jugs were hurled in his direction. He raised quite a commotion in medical and social circles until finally, in desperation, one doctor made the historical statement that "I would rather err with Galen than be right with Harvey!"

Man would have made an advance of exactly zero if this had always been the only method of testing evidence. But every so often during Man's progress, there have been rebels who were not satisfied with preponderance of opinion and who tested a fact for themselves, observing and accepting the data of their observation, and then testing again.

Possibly the first man who made a flint ax looked over a piece of flint and decided that the irregular stone could be chipped a certain way. When he found that flint would chip easily, he must have rushed to his tribe and enthusiastically tried to teach his fellow tribesmen how to make axes in the shape they desired instead of spending months searching for accidental pieces of stone of just the right shape. The chances are, he was stoned out of camp. Indulging in a further flight of fancy, it is not difficult to imagine that he finally managed to convince another fellow that his technique worked and that the two of them tied down a third with a piece of vine and forced him to watch them chip a flint ax from a rough stone. Finally, after convincing fifteen or twenty tribesmen by forceful demonstration, the followers of the new technique declared war on the rest of the tribe and, winning, forced the tribe to agree by decree.

EVALUATION OF DATA

Man has never known very much about that with which his mind is chiefly filled: data. What is data? What is the evaluation of data?

All these years in which psychoanalysis has taught its tenets to each generation of doctors, the authoritarian method was used, as can be verified by reading a few of the books on the subject. Within them is found, interminably, "Freud said…" The truly important thing is not that "Freud said" a thing, but "Is the data valuable? If it is valuable, how valuable is it?" You might say that a datum is as valuable as it has been evaluated. A datum can be proved in ratio to whether it can be evaluated by other data and its magnitude is established by how many other data it clarifies. Thus, the biggest datum possible would be one which would clarify and identify all knowledge known to Man in the material universe.

Unfortunately, however, there is no such thing as a Prime Datum. There must be not one datum, but two data, since a datum is of no use unless it can be evaluated. Furthermore, there must be a datum of similar magnitude with which to evaluate any given datum.

Data is *your* data only so long as *you* have evaluated it. It is your data by Authority or it is your data. If it is your data by Authority, somebody has forced it upon you. Of course, if you asked a question of a man whom you thought knew his business and he gave you his answer, that datum was not forced upon you. But if you went away from him believing from then on that such a datum existed without taking the trouble to investigate the answer for yourself–without comparing it to the known universe–you were falling short of completing the cycle of learning.

Mechanically, the major thing wrong with the mind is, of course, the turbulence in it. But the overburden of information in this society is enforced education that the individual has never been permitted to test. Literally, when you are told not to take anyone's word as an absolute datum, you are being asked to break a habit pattern forced upon you when you were a child. Your instructor in Scientology could have told you what he found to be true and invite you to test it for yourself. But unless you have tested it, you very likely do not have the fundamentals of Scientology in mind well enough to be comfortable in the use of any or all of the techniques available to you. This is why theory is so heavily stressed in Scientology. The instructor can tell you what he has found to be true and what others have found to be true, but at no time should he ask you to accept it. Please allow a plea otherwise: test it for yourself and convince yourself whether or not it exists as truth. And if you find that it does exist, you will be comfortable thereafter. Otherwise, unrecognized even by yourself, you are likely to find, down at the bottom of your information and education, an unresolved question which will itself undermine your ability to assimilate or practice anything in the line of a technique. Your mind will not be as facile on the subject as it should be.

Any quarrel you may have with theory is something that only you can resolve. Is the theory correct or isn't it correct? Only you can answer that. It cannot be answered for you. You can be told what others have achieved in the way of results and what others have observed, but you cannot become truly educated until you have achieved the results for yourself. The moment a man opens his mouth and asks, "Where is validation?" you can be sure you are looking at a very stupid man. That man is saying, bluntly and abruptly, "I cannot think for myself. I have to have Authority." Where could he possibly look for validation except into the physical universe and into his own subjective and objective reality?

A LOOK AT THE SCIENCES

Unfortunately, we are surrounded by a world that calls itself a world of science. But it is a world that is, in actuality, a world of Authority. True, that which is science today is far, far in advance of the Hindu concept of the world wherein a hemisphere rested on the backs of seven elephants which stood on seven pillars that stood on the back of a mud turtle, below which was mud into infinity.

The reason engineering and physics have reached out so far in advance of other sciences is the fact that they pose problems which punish Man so violently if he doesn't look carefully into the physical universe. An engineer is faced with the problem of drilling a tunnel through a mountain for a railroad. Tracks are laid up to the mountain on either side. If he judges space wrongly, the two tunnel entrances would fail to meet on the same level in the center. It would be so evident to one and all concerned that the engineer made a mistake that he takes great care not to make such a mistake. He observes the physical universe not only to the extent that the tunnel must meet to a fraction of an inch, but to the extent that if he were to misjudge wrongly the character of the rock through which he drills, the tunnel would cave in–an incident which would be considered a very unlucky and unfortunate occurrence to railroading.

Biology comes closer to being a science than some others because, in the field of biology, if someone makes too big a mistake about a bug, the immediate result can be dramatic and terrifying. Suppose a biologist is charged with the responsibility of injecting plankton into a water reservoir. Plankton are microscopic "germs" that are very useful to Man. But if, through some mistake, the biologist injects typhoid germs into the water supply, there would be an immediate and dramatic result.

Suppose a biologist is presented with the task of producing a culture of yeast which would, when placed in white bread dough, stain the bread brown. This man is up against the necessity of creating a yeast which not only behaves as yeast, but makes a dye as well. He has to deal with the practical aspect of the problem because, after he announces his success, there is the "yeast test": Is the bread edible? And the "brown bread test": Is the bread brown? Anyone could easily make the test and everyone would know very quickly whether or not the biologist had succeeded or failed.

Politics is called a science. There are natural laws about politics. They could be worked out if someone were to actually apply a scientific basis to political research.

In the field of humanities, science has been thoroughly adrift. Unquestioned, authoritarian principles have been followed.

Any person who accepts knowledge without questioning it and evaluating it for himself is demonstrating himself to be in apathy toward that sphere of knowledge.

FUNDAMENTALS

When a man tries to erect the plans of a lifetime or a profession on data which he himself has never evaluated, he cannot possibly succeed.

Fundamentals are very, very important, but first of all one must learn how to think in order to be absolutely sure of a fundamental. Thinking is not particularly hard to learn. It consists merely of comparing a particular datum with the physical universe as it is known and observed.

When there is an authoritarian basis for your education, you are not truly educated. Authoritarianism is little more than a form of hypnotism. Learning is forced under threat of some form of punishment. A student is stuffed with data which has not been individually evaluated, just as a taxidermist would stuff a snake. Such a student will be well informed and well educated according to present-day standards. But unfortunately, he will not be very successful in his chosen profession.

Indecision underlies an authoritarian statement. Do not allow your education to lie on the quicksand of indecision.

Examine the subject of Scientology on a very critical basis, not with the attitude that when you were in school you learned that such and such was true and since you learned that first, the first learning takes precedence.

Do not make the mistake of criticizing something on the basis of whether or not it concurs with the opinions of someone else.

The point which is pertinent is whether or not it concurs with *your* opinion. Does it agree with what *you* think?

Take the time and effort of making a complete examination of your subject, introspectively and by observation. The hard way is to sit down and memorize a million words–the method all too many educational systems employ in this age. Look at Scientology, study it, question it and use it and you will have discovered something for yourself. And in so doing, you might well discover a lot more. The techniques and the theories are highly workable, but they are not highly workable just because we say so!

So, the only advice I can give you is to study Scientology for itself and use it exactly as stated, then form your own opinions. Study it with the purpose in mind of arriving at your own conclusions as to whether the tenets you have assimilated are correct and workable. Compare what you have learned with the known universe. Seek for the reasons behind a manifestation, and postulate the manner and in which direction the manifestation will likely proceed. Do not allow the authority of any one person or school of thought to create a foregone conclusion within your sphere of knowledge.

Only with these principles of education in mind can you become a truly educated individual.

Man's Search for His Soul

Scientology:
A New Slant on Life

L. Ron Hubbard

" *I must face the fact*
that we have reached
that merger point where
science and religion meet,
and we must now cease
to pretend to deal with
material goals alone. "

MAN'S SEARCH FOR HIS SOUL

FOR COUNTLESS AGES PAST, Man has been engaged upon a search.

All thinkers in all ages have contributed their opinion and considerations to it. No scientist, no philosopher, no leader has failed to comment upon it. Billions of men have died for one opinion or another on the subject of this search. And no civilization, mighty or poor, in ancient or in modern times, has endured without battle on its account.

The human soul, to the civilized and barbaric alike, has been an endless source of interest, attention, hate or adoration.

To say that I have found the answer to all riddles of the soul would be inaccurate and presumptuous. To discount what I have come to know and to fail to make that known after observing its benefits would be a sin of omission against Man.

After decades of inquiry and thought and after years of public activity wherein I observed the material at work and its results, I can announce that in the knowledge I have developed, there must lie the answers to that riddle, to that enigma, to that problem–the human soul. For under my hands and others', I have seen the best in Man rehabilitated.

For the time since I first made a *Clear,* I have been, with some reluctance, out beyond any realm of the scientific known. I must face the fact that we have reached that merger point where science and religion meet, and we must now cease to pretend to deal with material goals alone.

We cannot deal in the realm of the human soul and ignore the fact. Man has too long pursued this search for its happy culmination here to be muffled by vague and scientific terms.

Religion, not science, has carried this search, this war, through the millennia. Science has all but swallowed Man with an ideology which denies the soul, a symptom of the failure of science in that search.

One cannot now play traitor to the men of God who sought these ages past to bring Man from the darkness.

We in Scientology belong in the ranks of the seekers after truth, not in the rear guard of the makers of the atom bomb.

However, science too has had its role in these endeavors. And nuclear physics, whatever crime it does against Man, may yet be redeemed by having been of aid in finding for Man the soul of which science had all but deprived him.

No Scientologist can easily close his eyes to the results he achieves today or fail to see them superior to the materialistic technologies he earlier used. For we can know, with all else we know, that the human soul, freed, is the only effective therapeutic agent that we have. But our goals, no matter our miracles with bodies today, exceed physical health and better men.

Scientology is the science of knowing how to know. It has taught us that a man *is* his own immortal soul. And it gives us little choice but to announce to a world, no matter how it receives it, that nuclear physics and religion have joined hands and that we in Scientology perform those miracles for which Man through all his search has hoped.

The individual may hate God or despise priests. He cannot ignore, however, the evidence that he is his own soul. Thus we have resolved our riddle and found the answer simple.

L. RON HUBBARD

ON THE MIND AND
SURVIVAL

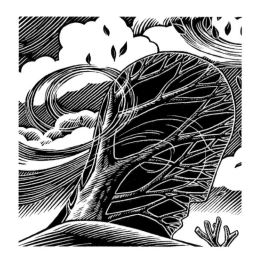

ON OUR EFFORTS
FOR IMMORTALITY

SCIENTOLOGY:
A NEW SLANT ON LIFE

L. RON HUBBARD

" Life is an interdependent,
cooperative effort. Each and every
living organism has a part to play in
the survival of other organisms. "

ON OUR EFFORTS
FOR IMMORTALITY

THE PHYSICAL UNIVERSE consists of four elements–*matter, energy, space and time.*

According to nuclear physics, matter is composed of energy such as electrons and protons. And the energy and the matter exist in space and time. All this is actually very simple. And even then we need not go very far into it to understand that the universe in which we live is composed of simple things arranged and rearranged to make many forms and manifestations.

The concrete sidewalk, the air, ice-cream sodas, paychecks, cats, kings and coal heavers are basically composed of matter, energy, space and time. And where they are alive, they contain another ingredient–*life.*

Life is an energy of a very special kind, obeying certain laws different from what we normally consider energy (such as electricity). But life is an energy and it has some peculiar properties.

Life is able to collect and organize matter and energy in space and time and animate it. Life takes some matter and energy and makes an organism such as a monocell, a tree, a polar bear or a man.

Then this organism, still animated by the energy called life, further acts upon matter and energy in space and time and further organizes and animates matter and energy into new objects and shapes.

Life could be said to be engaged upon a conquest of the physical universe. The primary urge of life has been said to be SURVIVAL! In order to accomplish survival, life has to continue and win in its conquest of the physical universe.

When life or a life form ceases to continue that conquest, it ceases to survive and succumbs.

Here we have a gigantic action. The energy of life versus matter, energy, space and time. Life versus the physical universe.

Here is an enormous struggle. The chaotic, disorganized physical universe, capable only of force, resisting the conquest of life, organizing and persistent, capable of reason.

Life learns the laws of the physical universe—matter, energy, space and time—and then turns those laws against the physical universe to further its conquest.

Man has spent much time learning what he could of the physical universe as in the sciences of physics and chemistry, but more important even, of the daily battle of life against the universe. Do not think that a monocell does not manifest a knowledge of life's working rules, for it does. What cunning it takes to organize some chemicals and sunlight into a living unit! The biologist stands in awe of the expertness of management of the smallest living cells. He gazes at these intricate and careful entities, these microscopic units of life forms, and even he cannot believe that it is all an accident.

There is life, then, a vital energy, not quite like physical universe energy. And then there are life forms.

The life form or the organism, such as a *living* human body, consists of life *plus* physical universe matter, energy, space and time. A *dead* body consists of physical universe matter, energy, space and time *minus* life energy. Life has been there, has organized and has then withdrawn from the organism, an operation we know as the cycle of conception, birth, growth, decay and death.

Although there are answers as to where life goes when it withdraws and what it then does, we need not examine that now. The important thing to a living organism is the fact that it is seeking to survive, in obedience to the whole effort of all life, and that in order to do so it must succeed in its conquest of the physical universe.

Stated simply, life must first accumulate enough matter and energy to make up an organism (such as the human body) and must then ally the organism with friendly and cooperative organisms (such as other people) and must continue to procure additional matter and energy for food, clothing and shelter in order to support itself. Additionally, in order to survive, it must do two specific things which, beyond the necessity of allies, food, clothing and shelter, are basically important.

Life must procure pleasure.

Life must avoid pain.

Life has an active thrust away from pain, which is non-survival, destructive and which is death itself. Pain is a warning of non-survival or potential death.

Life has an active thrust toward pleasure. Pleasure can be defined as the action toward obtaining or the procurement of survival. The ultimate pleasure is an infinity of survival or immortality–a goal unobtainable for the physical organism itself (but not its life), but toward which the organism strives.

Happiness, then, could be defined as the overcoming of obstacles toward a desirable goal. Any desirable goal, if closely inspected, will be found to be a survival goal.

Too much pain obstructs the organism toward survival.

Too many obstructions between the organism and survival mean non-survival.

Thus one finds the mind engaged in computing or imagining ways and means to avoid pain and reach pleasure and putting the solutions into action. And this is all that the mind does:

It perceives, poses and resolves problems relating to the survival of the organism, the future generations, the group, life and the physical universe and puts the solutions into action.

If it solves the majority of the problems presented, the organism thus achieves a high level of survival. If the organism's mind fails to resolve a majority of problems, then the organism fails.

The mind, then, has a definite relationship to survival. And one means here the whole mind, not just the brain. The brain is a structure. The mind can be considered to be the whole being, mortal and immortal, the definite personality of the organism and all its attributes.

Hence, if one's mind is working well, if it is resolving the problems it should resolve and if it is putting those solutions into proper action, the survival of the organism is well assured. If the mind is not working well, the survival of the organism is thrown into question and doubt.

One's mind, then, must be in excellent condition if he is to best guarantee the survival of himself, his family, future generations, his group and life.

The mind seeks to guarantee and direct survival actions. It seeks survival not only for the organism (self) but seeks it for the family, children, future generations and all life. Thus it can be selectively blunted. A mind can be blunted concerning the survival of self and yet be alive to the survival of future generations. It can be blunted concerning groups and yet be very alive to its responsibility for the organism (self). In order to function well, the mind must not be blunted in any direction.

To function well, the mind must conceive itself able to handle the physical universe of matter, energy, space and time within the necessities of the organism, the family, future generations and groups as well as life.

The mind must be able to avoid pain for and discover pleasure for the self, future generations, the family and the group as well as life itself.

As the mind fails to avoid pain and discover pleasure, so fails the organism, the family, future generations, the group and life.

The failure of one organism in a group to properly resolve survival problems is a failure, in part, for the whole group. Hence, "Do not send to find for whom the bell tolls, it tolls for thee!"

Life is an interdependent, cooperative effort. Each and every living organism has a part to play in the survival of other organisms.

When it comes to a thinking mind such as Man's, the organism must be able to act independently for its own survival and the survival of others. In order to accomplish these survivals, however, a mind has to be able to realize solutions which are optimum not only for self, but for all other things concerned in its survival.

Thus the mind of one organism must reach agreements with the minds of other organisms in order that all may survive to the highest possible level.

When a mind becomes dulled and blunted, it begins to compute its solutions poorly. It begins to get confused about its goals. It is not sure what it really means to do. And it will involve and inhibit the survival of other organisms. It may begin, for instance, to compute that it must survive as self and that only self is important and so neglect the survival of others. This is non-survival activity. It is highly aberrated.

A mind which begins to "survive" only for self, and begins to diminish and control with force other organisms around, is already better than halfway toward its own death. It is a mind which is less than half alive. It has less than half its actual potential. Its perception of the physical universe is poor. It does not realize that it is dependent for survival upon cooperation with others. It has lost its survival mission. This mind is already outward bound toward death, has passed its peak and will actually take personal actions which lead to its own death.

Life, the large overall life, has a use for organism death. When an organism can no longer continue well, the plan of life is to kill it and invest anew in a new organism.

Death is life's operation of disposing of an outmoded and unwanted organism so that new organisms can be born and can flourish.

Life itself does not die. Only the physical organism dies. Not even a personality, apparently, dies. Death, then, in truth, is a limited concept of the death of the physical part of the organism. Life and the personality, apparently, go on. The physical part of the organism ceases to function. And that is death.

When an organism reaches a point where it is only half conscious, where it is only perceiving half as well as it should, where it is functioning only half as well as it should, death begins. The organism, thereafter, will take actions to hasten death. It does this "unconsciously." But in its aberrated state, such a mind will also bring death to other organisms. Thus a half-conscious organism is a menace to others. Here is the accident-prone, the fascist, the person who seeks to dominate, the selfish and self-seeking person. Here is an organism outward bound.

When an organism reaches a point where it is only a third alive, a third conscious, it is perceiving only a third of what it might. Life even further hastens the death of this organism and those around it. Here is the suicide, here is the person who is continually ill, who refuses to eat.

Organisms which are outward bound toward death sometimes require years and years to die. For the organism experiences resurgences and still has some small desire to go on living. And other organisms help it to live. It is carried along by the tide of life even though its individual direction is toward death – death for others and death for self and death for the physical universe around it.

Society, the bulk of which is bent upon survival, fails or refuses to recognize death or the urge of organisms toward it. Society passes laws against murder and suicide. Society provides hospitals. Society carries such people upon its back. And society will not hear of euthanasia or "mercy killing."

Organisms which have passed the halfway point will take extraordinary measures and means to bring about death for others and for things and for self. Here we have the Hitlers, the criminals, the destructively neurotic.

Give a person who has passed this point a car to drive and the car may become involved in an accident. Give him money and the money will go to purchase non-survival things.

But we must not emphasize the dramatic and forget the important like the newspapers do. The action and urge toward death becomes noticeable only when it is very dramatic. It is most dangerous, however, in its undramatic forms.

A person who has passed the halfway point brings death to things and people on a small scale at all times. A house left dirty, appointments not kept, clothing not cared for, vicious gossip, carping criticisms of others "for their own good"–these are all enturbulences which bring failure and too many failures bring death.

And it should not be supposed that by "halfway point," one means halfway through life. It means half conscious, half alive, half (or less) perceiving and thinking. A child may be suppressed to this level by his parents and school. And, indeed, children quite ordinarily drop below the halfway point, so defeated do they become in their environment and in their contest with life. Age is no criterion. But physical health is.

The surest manifestation that someone has passed the halfway point is his physical condition. The chronically ill have passed it.

If one is to have a secure society, then, if one is to rid a society of its death factors, one must have some means of either destroying the people who bring death to it–the Hitlers, the insane, the criminals–or he must have some means of salvaging these people and bringing them back into a state of full consciousness.

Full consciousness would mean full recognition of one's responsibilities, his relationship with others, his care of himself and of society.

How can such a thing be achieved? If you could achieve it, you could raise a social order to hitherto unattainable heights. You could empty the prisons and insane asylums. You could make a world too sane for war. And people could be made well who have never had the means of it before. And people could be happy who have never truly known what happiness was. You could raise the goodwill and efficiency of all men and all social orders if you could restore the vitality of these people.

In order to know how it can be restored, one has to know how the consciousness, the vitality and the will to live become reduced.

ON RAISING OUR LEVEL
OF CONSCIOUSNESS

SCIENTOLOGY:
A NEW SLANT ON LIFE

L. RON HUBBARD

" The vitality
of living, of seeking
higher levels of survival,
is life itself. "

On Raising Our Level of Consciousness

An organism is suppressed toward death by accumulated pain.

Pain in one great sweeping shock brings about immediate death.

Pain in small doses over a lifetime gradually suppresses the organism toward death.

What is pain?

Pain is the warning of loss. It is an automatic alarm system built into life organisms which informs the organism that some part of it or all of it is under stress and that the organism had better take action or die.

The signal of pain means that the organism is in the proximity of a destructive force or object. To ignore pain is to die. Pain is the whip which sends the organism away from hot stoves, sub-zero weather. Pain is the threat of non-survival, the punishment for errors in trying to survive.

And pain is always loss. A burned finger means that the body has lost the cells on the surface of that finger. They are dead. A blow on the head means the death of scalp and other cells in the area. The whole organism is thus warned of the proximity of a death source and so attempts to get away from it.

The loss of a loved one is also a loss of survival. The loss of a possession is also loss of survival potential. One then confuses physical pain and the loss of survival organisms or objects. And so there is such a thing as "mental pain."

But life, in its whole contest with the physical universe, has no patience with failure. An organism so foolhardy as to let itself be struck too hard and so depressed into unconsciousness stays in the vicinity of the pain-dealing object. It is considered to be non-survival if it fails so markedly to survive.

Unconsciousness experienced as a result of a blow or an illness is a quick picture of what happens over a life span.

Is there any difference, except time, between these two things?

A blow resulting in unconsciousness which results in death.

The accumulated blows over a life span resulting in a gradual lessening of consciousness resulting in eventual death.

One is slower than the other.

One of the basic discoveries was that unconsciousness and all the pain attendant upon it were stored in a part of the mind and that this pain and unconsciousness accumulated until they caused the organism to begin to die.

Another discovery was that this pain could be nullified or erased with a return to full consciousness and a rehabilitation toward survival.

In other words, it became possible to cancel out the accumulated unconsciousness and pain of the years and restore the health and vitality of an organism.

Accumulated physical pain and loss bring about a reduction of consciousness, a reduction of physical health and a reduction of the will to live to a point where the organism actively, if often slyly, seeks death.

Erase or nullify the physical pain, the losses of a lifetime, and vitality returns.

The vitality of living, of seeking higher levels of survival, is life itself.

The human body was found to be extremely capable of repairing itself when the stored memories of pain were cancelled. Further, it was discovered that so long as the stored pain remained, the doctoring of what are called psychosomatic ills, such as arthritis, rheumatism, dermatitis and thousands of others, could not result in anything permanent. Psychotherapy, not knowing about pain storage and its effects, discovered long ago that one could rid a patient of one illness only to have another pop up. And psychotherapy became a defeatist school because it could do nothing permanent for the aberrated or the ill, even when it could do a little something to relieve it. Hence, *all* efforts to make men vital and well became suspect because the reason they were inefficient and ill had not been discovered and proven.

With these new discoveries, it became possible to eradicate aberration and illness because it became possible to nullify or eradicate the pain from the pain-storage banks of the body without applying further pain, as in surgery.

Consciousness, then, depends upon the absence or the nullification or eradication of memories of physical pain, for unconsciousness is a part of that pain–one of its symptoms.

Arthritis of the knee, for instance, is the accumulation of all knee injuries in the past. The body confuses time and environment with the time and environment where the knee was actually injured and so keeps the pain there. The fluids of the body avoid the pain area. Hence, a deposit which is called arthritis. The proof of this is that when the knee injuries of the past are located and discharged, the arthritis ceases, no other injury takes its place and the person is finished with arthritis of the knee. And this happens ten cases out of ten–except in those cases where age and physical deterioration are so well advanced toward death that the point of no return is passed.

Take a bad heart. The person has pain in his heart. He can take medicine or voodoo or another diet and still have a bad heart. Find and eradicate or nullify an actual physical injury to the heart and the heart ceases to hurt and gets well.

Nothing is easier to prove than these tenets. A good auditor (Scientology practitioner) can take a broken-down, sorrow-drenched lady of thirty-eight and knock out her past periods of physical and mental pain and have on his hands somebody who appears to be twenty-five–and a bright, cheerful twenty-five at that.

Sure it's incredible. But so is an A-bomb, a few pennyweights of plutonium, which can blow a city off the chart.

Once you know the basic tenets of life and how it acts as an energy, life can be put back into the ill, the devitalized, the would-be suicide.

And more important than treating the very ill, mentally or physically, one can interrupt the downward spiral in a man who is still alert and well so that he will not thereafter become so ill. And one can take the so-called normal person and send his state of being up to levels of brilliance and success not possible before.

Restore an individual's full consciousness and you restore his full life potential.

And it can now be done.

L. Ron Hubbard

On the Fundamentals of Life and Living

THE
EIGHT DYNAMICS

SCIENTOLOGY:
A NEW SLANT ON LIFE

L. RON HUBBARD

" *As one looks out across the confusion which is life or existence to most people, one can discover eight main divisions.* "

The
Eight Dynamics

As one looks out across the confusion which is life or existence to most people, one can discover eight main divisions.

There could be said to be eight urges (drives, impulses) in life.

These we call *dynamics*.

These are motives or motivations.

We call them *the eight dynamics*.

There is no thought or statement here that any one of these eight dynamics is more important than the others. While they are categories (divisions) of the broad game of life, they are not necessarily equal to each other. It will be found amongst individuals that each person stresses one of the dynamics more than the others, or may stress a combination of dynamics as more important than other combinations.

The purpose in setting forth this division is to increase an understanding of life by placing it in compartments. Having subdivided existence in this fashion, each compartment can be inspected (as itself and by itself) in its relationship to the other compartments of life.

In working a puzzle, it is necessary to first take pieces of similar color or character and place them in groups. In studying a subject, it is necessary to proceed in an orderly fashion.

To promote this orderliness, it is necessary to assume (for our purposes) these eight arbitrary compartments of life.

The First Dynamic is the urge toward existence as one's self. Here we have individuality expressed fully. This can be called the *Self Dynamic*.

The Second Dynamic is the urge toward existence as a sexual activity. This dynamic actually has two divisions. Second Dynamic (a) is the sexual act itself. And the Second Dynamic (b) is the family unit, including the rearing of children. This can be called the *Sex Dynamic*.

The Third Dynamic is the urge toward existence in groups of individuals. Any group, or part of an entire class, could be considered to be a part of the Third Dynamic. The school, the society, the town, the nation are each *part* of the Third Dynamic and each one *is* a Third Dynamic. This can be called the *Group Dynamic*.

The Fourth Dynamic is the urge toward existence as or of Mankind. Whereas one race would be considered a Third Dynamic, all the races would be considered the Fourth Dynamic. This can be called the *Mankind Dynamic*.

The Fifth Dynamic is the urge toward existence of the animal kingdom. This includes all living things, whether vegetable or animal, the fish in the sea, the beasts of the field or of the forest, grass, trees, flowers or anything directly and intimately motivated by *life*. This can be called the *Animal Dynamic*.

The Sixth Dynamic is the urge toward existence as the physical universe. The physical universe is composed of Matter, Energy, Space and Time. In Scientology we take the first letter of each of these words and coin a word—MEST. This can be called the *Universe Dynamic*.

The Seventh Dynamic is the urge toward existence as or of spirits. Anything spiritual, with or without identity, would come under the heading of the Seventh Dynamic. This can be called the *Spiritual Dynamic*.

The Eighth Dynamic is the urge toward existence as infinity. This is also identified as the Supreme Being. This is called the Eighth Dynamic because the symbol of infinity, ∞, stood upright makes the numeral 8. This can be called the *Infinity* or *God Dynamic*.

Scientologists usually call these by number.

A further manifestation of these dynamics is that they could best be represented as a series of concentric circles, wherein the First Dynamic would be the center and each new dynamic would be successively a circle outside it.

The basic characteristic of the individual includes his ability to so expand into the other dynamics.

As an example of use of these dynamics, one discovers that a baby at birth is not perceptive beyond the First Dynamic. But as the child grows and interests extend, the child can be seen to embrace other dynamics.

As a further example of use, a person who is incapable of operating on the Third Dynamic is incapable at once of being a part of a team and so might be said to be incapable of a social existence.

As a further comment upon the eight dynamics, no one of these dynamics from one to seven is more important than any other one of them in terms of orienting the individual.

The abilities and shortcomings of individuals can be understood by viewing their participation in the various dynamics.

THE
AFFINITY, REALITY AND
COMMUNICATION TRIANGLE

SCIENTOLOGY:
A NEW SLANT ON LIFE

L. RON HUBBARD

" The A-R-C Triangle is the keystone of living associations. This triangle is the common denominator to all of life's activities. "

THE
AFFINITY, REALITY AND
COMMUNICATION TRIANGLE

THERE IS A TRIANGLE of considerable importance in Scientology, and an ability to use it gives a much greater understanding of life.

The *A-R-C Triangle* is the keystone of living associations. This triangle is the common denominator to all of life's activities.

The first corner of the triangle is called *affinity*.

The basic definition of affinity is "the consideration of distance, whether good or bad." The most basic function of complete affinity would be the ability to occupy the same space as something else.

The word affinity is here used to mean "love, liking or any other emotional attitude." Affinity is conceived in Scientology to be something of many facets. Affinity is a variable quality. Affinity is here used as a word with the context "degree of liking."

Under affinity we have the various emotional tones, ranged from the highest to the lowest, and these are in part:

Serenity — (the highest level)

Enthusiasm

Conservatism — (as we proceed downward towards the baser affinities)

Boredom

Antagonism

Anger

Covert Hostility

Fear

Grief

Apathy

(This, in Scientology, is called the *Tone Scale*.)

Below Apathy, affinity proceeds into solidities such as matter. Affinity is conceived to be comprised first of thought, then of emotion which contains energy particles, and then as a solid.

The second corner of the triangle is *reality*.

Reality could be defined as "that which appears to be." Reality is fundamentally agreement. What we agree to be real is real.

The third corner of the triangle is *communication*.

In understanding the composition of human relations in this universe, communication is more important than the other two corners of the triangle. Communication is the solvent for all things (it dissolves all things).

The interrelationship of the triangle becomes apparent at once when one asks, "Have you ever tried to talk to an angry man?" Without a high degree of liking and without some basis of agreement, there is no *communication*. Without communication and some basis of emotional response, there can be no *reality*. Without some basis for agreement and communication, there can be no *affinity*. Thus we call these three things a *triangle*. Unless we have two corners of a triangle, there cannot be a third corner. Desiring any corner of the triangle, one must include the other two.

The triangle is conceived to be very spacious at the level of Serenity and completely condensed at the level of matter. Thus, to represent a scale for use, one would draw a large triangle with the high part of the scale and succeedingly smaller triangles down to a dot at the bottom of the scale.

Affinity, Reality and Communication are the basis of the Scientology Tone Scale which gives a prediction of human behavior.

As has already been noted, the triangle is not an equilateral (all sides the same) triangle. Affinity and reality are very much less important than communication. It might be said that the triangle begins with communication which brings into existence affinity and reality.

A-R-C are *understanding*.

If you would continue a strong and able communication with someone, there must be some basis for agreement, there must be some liking for the person and then communication can exist. We can see, then, that simple "talking" and "writing" randomly, without knowledge of this, would not necessarily be communication. Communication is essentially "something which is sent and which is received." The intention to send and the intention to receive must both be present, in some degree, before an actual communication can take place. Therefore, one could have conditions which appear to be communications which were not.

Original with Scientology (as are all these concepts), the A-R-C Triangle, understood, is an extremely useful tool or weapon in human relationships. For instance, amongst the A-R-C Triangle laws, a communication to be received must approximate the affinity level of the person to whom it is directed. As people descend the Tone Scale, they become more and more difficult to communicate with and things with which they will agree become more and more solid. Thus, we have friendly discourses high on the scale and war at the bottom. Where the affinity level is hate, the agreement is solid matter, and the communication...*bullets*.

THE REASON WHY

SCIENTOLOGY:
A NEW SLANT ON LIFE

L. RON HUBBARD

" Although Man continually uses 'Freedom!' for his war cry, he only succeeds in establishing further entrapment for himself. The reason for this is a very simple one. "

The Reason Why

LIFE CAN BEST be understood by likening it to a *game*.

Since we are exterior to a great number of games, we can regard them with a detached eye. If we were exterior to life, instead of being involved and immersed in the living of it, it would look to us much like games look to us from our present vantage point.

Despite the amount of suffering, pain, misery, sorrow and travail which can exist in life, the reason for existence is the same reason as one has to play a game–interest, contest, activity and possession. The truth of this assertion is established by an observation of the elements of games and then applying these elements to life itself. When we do this, we find nothing left wanting in the panorama of life.

By game we mean "contest of person against person, or team against team." When we say games, we mean such games as baseball, polo, chess or any other such pastime.

It may at one time have struck you peculiar that men would risk bodily injury in the field of play, just for the sake of "amusement." So it might strike you as peculiar that people would go on living or would enter into the "game of life," at the risk of all the sorrow, travail and pain, just to have "something to do." Evidently there is no greater curse than total idleness. Of course, there is that condition where a person continues to play a game in which he is no longer interested.

If you will but look about the room and check off items in which you are not interested, you will discover something remarkable. In a short time, you will find that there is nothing in the room in which you are not interested. You are interested in everything. However, disinterest itself is one of the mechanisms of play. In order to hide something, it is only necessary to make everyone disinterested in the place where the item is hidden. Disinterest is not an immediate result of interest which has worn out. Disinterest is a commodity in itself. It is palpable. It exists.

By studying the elements of games, we find ourselves in possession of the elements of life.

Life is a game.

A game consists of *freedom, barriers* and *purposes*.

This is a scientific fact, not merely an observation.

Freedom exists amongst barriers. A totality of barriers and a totality of freedom, alike, are "no-game conditions." Each is similarly cruel. Each is similarly purposeless.

Great revolutionary movements fail. They promise unlimited freedom. That is the road to failure. Only stupid visionaries chant of endless freedom. Only the afraid and ignorant speak of and insist upon unlimited barriers.

When the relation between freedom and barriers becomes too unbalanced, an unhappiness results.

"Freedom from" is all right only so long as there is a place to be free *to*. An endless desire for "freedom from" is a perfect trap, a fear of all things.

Barriers are composed of inhibiting (limiting) ideas, space, energy, masses and time. Freedom, in its entirety, would be a total absence of these things. But it would also be a freedom without thought or action–an unhappy condition of total nothingness.

Fixed on too many barriers, Man yearns to be free. But launched into total freedom, he is purposeless and miserable.

There is "freedom amongst" barriers. If the barriers are known and the freedoms are known, there can be life, living, happiness, a game.

The restrictions of a government or a job give an employee his freedom. Without known restrictions, an employee is a slave doomed to the fears of uncertainty in all his actions.

Executives in business and government can fail in three ways and thus bring about a chaos in their department. They can:

1. Seem to give endless freedom.
2. Seem to give endless barriers.
3. Make neither freedom nor barriers certain.

Executive competence, therefore, consists of imposing and enforcing an adequate balance between their people's freedom and the unit's barriers *and* in being precise and consistent about those freedoms and barriers. Such an executive, adding only in himself initiative and purpose, can have a department with initiative and purpose.

An employee buying and/or insisting upon "freedom only" will become a slave. Knowing the above facts, he must insist upon a workable balance between freedom and barriers.

An examination of the dynamics will demonstrate the possibility of a combination of teams. Two Group Dynamics can engage one another as teams. The Self Dynamic can ally itself with the Animal Dynamic against, let us say, the Universe Dynamic and so have a game. In other words, the dynamics are an outline of possible teams and interplays. As everyone is engaged in several games, an examination of the dynamics will plot and clarify for him the various teams he is playing upon and those he is playing against. If an individual can discover that he is only playing on the Self Dynamic and that he belongs to no other team, it is certain that this individual will lose. For he has before him seven remaining dynamics and the Self Dynamic is seldom capable of besting, by itself, all the remaining dynamics. In Scientology, we call this condition the "only one." Here is Self-determinism in the guise of *Selfish*-determinism. And here is an individual who will most certainly be overwhelmed. To enjoy life, one must be willing to be some part of life.

There is the principle in Scientology called *Pan-determinism*.

This could be loosely defined as "determining the activities of two or more sides in a game simultaneously."

For instance, a person playing chess is being Self-determined and is playing chess against an opponent. A person who is Pan-determined on the subject of chess could play both sides of the board.

A being is Pan-determined about any game to which he is *senior*. He is Self-determined only in a game to which he is *junior*.

For instance, a general of an army is Pan-determined concerning an argument between two privates or even two companies of his command. He is Pan-determined in this case. But when he confronts another army, led by another general, he becomes Self-determined. The game, in this wise, could be said to be *larger* than himself. The game becomes even larger than this when the general seeks to play the parts of all the political heads which should be above him. This is the main reason why dictatorship doesn't work. It is all but impossible for one man to be Pan-determined about the entire system of games which comprise a nation. He starts "taking sides" and then, to that degree, becomes much *less* than the government which he is seeking to run.

It has been stylish in past ages to insist only upon freedom. The French Revolution furnishes an excellent example for this. In the late part of the eighteenth century, the nobles of France became so Self-determined against the remainder of the country, and were so incapable of taking the parts of the populace, that the nobles were destroyed. Immediately, the populace itself sought to take over the government. And being untrained and being intensely antipathetic to any and all restraints, their war cry became "Freedom!" They had no further restrictions or barriers. The rules of government were thrown aside. Theft and brigandage took the place of economics. The populace, therefore, found itself in a deeper trap and discovered itself to be involved with a dictatorship which was far more restrictive than anything they had experienced before the revolution.

Although Man continually uses "Freedom!" for his war cry, he only succeeds in establishing further entrapment for himself. The reason for this is a very simple one. A game consists of freedom *and* barriers *and* purposes. When Man drops the idea of restrictions or barriers, he loses at once *control* over barriers. He becomes Self-determined about barriers and not Pan-determined. Thus, he cannot control the barriers. The barriers, left uncontrolled, trap him then and there.

The "dwindling spiral" comes about directly when Man shuns barriers. If he considers all restrictions and barriers his enemies, he is of course refusing to control them in any way and thus he starts his own dwindling spiral.

A race which is educated to think in terms of "freedom only" is very easily entrapped. No one in the nation will take responsibility for restrictions. Therefore, restrictions apparently become less and less. Actually, they become more and more. As these restrictions lessen, so lessens the freedom of the individual. One cannot be free from a wall unless there is a wall. Lacking any restrictions, life becomes purposeless, random, chaotic.

A good manager must be capable of taking responsibility for restrictions. In that freedom, to exist, must have barriers, a failure to take initiative on the subject of restrictions or barriers causes them to arise all by themselves and exist without consent or direction.

There are various states of mind which bring about happiness. That state of mind which insists only upon freedom can bring about nothing but unhappiness. It would be better to develop a thought pattern which looked for new ways to be entrapped and things to be trapped in, than to suffer the eventual total entrapment of dwelling upon "freedom only." A man who is willing to accept restrictions and barriers and is not afraid of them is *free*. A man who does nothing but fight restrictions and barriers will usually be *trapped*. The way to have endless war is "abandon" all war.

As it can be seen in any game, purposes become counterposed. There is a matter of purpose-counter-purpose in almost any game played in a field with two teams. One team has the idea of reaching the goal of the other, and the other has the idea of reaching the goal of the first. Their purposes are at war and this warring of purposes makes a game.

The war of purposes gives us what we call *problems.*

A problem has the anatomy of purposes. A problem consists of two or more purposes opposed. It does not matter what problem you face or have faced, the basic anatomy of that problem is purpose-counter-purpose.

In actual testing, in Scientology, it has been discovered that a person begins to suffer from problems when he does not have enough of them. There is the old saw (maxim) that if you want a thing done, give it to a busy man to do. Similarly, if you want a happy associate, make sure that he is a man who can have lots of problems.

From this we get the oddity of a high incidence of neurosis in the families of the rich. These people have very little to do and have very few problems. The basic problems of food, clothing and shelter are already solved for them. We would suppose, then, if it were true that an individual's happiness depended only upon his freedom, these people would be happy. However, they are not happy. What brings about their unhappiness? It is the lack of problems.

Although successful processing in Scientology would depend upon taking all three elements of games into consideration (and, indeed, that is the secret of bettering people—taking freedom, barriers and purposes into consideration and balancing them), it is true that you could make a man well simply by sitting down

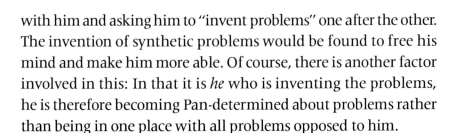

with him and asking him to "invent problems" one after the other. The invention of synthetic problems would be found to free his mind and make him more able. Of course, there is another factor involved in this: In that it is *he* who is inventing the problems, he is therefore becoming Pan-determined about problems rather than being in one place with all problems opposed to him.

One who is plotting continually how to "get out of things" will become miserable. One who is plotting how to "get into things" has a much better chance of becoming happy.

There is, of course, the matter of being forced to play games in which one has no interest. A war into which one is drafted is an excellent example of this. One is not interested in the purposes of the war and yet one finds himself fighting it. Thus there must be an additional element.

And this element is *the power of choice*.

One could say, then, that life is a game and that the ability to play a game consists of tolerance for freedom and barriers and an insight into purposes with the power of choice over participation.

These four elements–*freedom, barriers, purposes* and *power of choice*–are the guiding elements of life.

This, then, is the broad picture of life. And in bringing life into focus and in making it less confusing, these elements are used in its understanding.

L. RON HUBBARD

ON WORK AND SUCCESS

HANDLING THE CONFUSIONS OF THE WORKADAY WORLD

SCIENTOLOGY:
A NEW SLANT ON LIFE

L. RON HUBBARD

" Confusion is the basic cause of
stupidity. To the stupid,
all things except the very simple
ones are confused. Thus, if one knew
the anatomy of confusion,
no matter how bright one might
be, he would be brighter. "

HANDLING THE CONFUSIONS
OF THE WORKADAY WORLD

ONE MIGHT BE LED to believe there was something confusing about navigating one's career in the world of work. And confusion there is to one who is not equipped with guides and maps.

Basically, it all seemed very simple, this thing called work, getting a job. One was educated into some skill and one read an ad or was sent by a friend and was interviewed for a job. And one got it and then reported every day and did the things assigned and, as time went on, hoped for a raise in pay. And time going even further on brought one to hope for a pension or a governmental regime that would pay old-age benefits. And that was the simple pattern of it.

But times change and simple patterns have a habit of being deranged. The various incidents and accidents of fate entered into the picture. Completely aside from personal factors, larger views alter things. The government in sweeping economy fails to grant adequate pension. The business for which one works is shattered by a time of depression. Or one's health fails inexplicably and one is left on charity.

The worker in his workaday world is no towering giant amongst his many foes. The "tinsel path" sketched so happily by "rabble-rousers," the great affection held for the worker by this or that ideology or political figure, do not reflect fact. A man working at a job is faced by difficulties large enough to him, no matter how small they might seem to a successful industrialist. A few percent rise in taxes may mean that he thereafter goes without simple pleasures. An entrance upon bad times for the business may result in lessened pay, and there may go any and all luxuries and even some necessities–or the job.

The effect of international currents, governments, business trends and markets all usually beyond his concern, the worker is perfectly entitled to believe that his fate is not quite entirely predictable. Indeed, he might even be entitled to be confused.

A man can starve to death in a few days. Few workers have many days of margin in their pockets if the currents change. Thus many things, which would be no vast problem to the very secure, are watched as menaces by the worker. And these things can become so many that all life seems too confused to be borne and one sinks into an apathy of day-to-day grind, without much hope, trusting that the next storm, by luck, will pass over him.

As one looks at the many factors which might derange his life and undermine his security, the impression of "confusion" seems well founded. And it can be said, with truth, that all difficulties are fundamentally confusions. Given enough menace, enough unknown, a man ducks his head and tries to swing through it blindly. He has been overcome by confusions.

Enough unsolved problems add up to a huge confusion. Every now and then, on his job, enough conflicting orders bring the worker into a state of confusion. A modern plant can be so poorly managed that the entire thing appears to be a vast confusion to which no answer is possible.

Luck is the usual answer one resorts to in a confusion. If the forces about one seem too great, one can always "rely on his luck." By luck we mean "destiny not personally guided." When one turns loose an automobile wheel and hopes the car will stay on the road, by luck, he is often disappointed. And so it is in life. Those things left to chance become less likely to work themselves out.

One has seen a friend shutting his eyes to the bill collectors and gritting his teeth while he hopes that he will win at the races and solve all his problems. One has known people who handled their lives this way for years. Indeed, one of Dickens' great characters had the entire philosophy of "waiting for something to turn up." But luck, while we grant that it *is* a potent element, is only necessary amid a strong current of confusing factors. If one has to have *luck* to see him through, then it follows that one isn't any longer at his own automobile wheel. And it follows, too, that one is dealing with a confusion.

A confusion can be defined as "any set of factors or circumstances which do not seem to have any immediate solution."

More broadly:

A confusion in this universe is random motion.

If you were to stand in heavy traffic, you would be likely to feel confused by all the motion whizzing around you. If you were to stand in a heavy storm with leaves and papers flying by, you would be likely to feel confused.

Is it possible to actually understand a confusion? Is there any such thing as an "anatomy of confusion"? Yes, there is.

If, as a switchboard operator, you had ten calls hitting your board at once, you might feel confused. But is there any answer to the situation?

If, as a shop foreman, you have three emergencies and an accident all at the same time, you might feel confused. But is there any answer to that?

A confusion is only a confusion so long as *all* particles are in motion. A confusion is only a confusion so long as *no* factor is clearly defined or understood.

Confusion is the basic cause of stupidity. To the stupid, all things except the very simple ones are confused. Thus, if one knew the anatomy of confusion, no matter how bright one might be, he would be brighter.

If you have ever had to teach some young aspirant who was not too bright, you will understand this well. You attempt to explain how such-and-so works. You go over it and over it and over it. And then you turn him loose and he promptly makes a complete botch of it. He "didn't understand," he "didn't grasp it." You can simplify your understanding of his misunderstanding by saying, very rightly, "He was confused."

Ninety-nine percent of all education fails, when it fails, on the grounds that the student was confused. And not only in the realm of the job, but in life itself. When failure approaches, it is born, one way or another, from confusion. To learn of machinery or to live life, one has to be able either to stand up to confusion or to take it apart.

We have, in Scientology, a certain doctrine about confusion. It is called:

The Doctrine of the Stable Datum.

If you saw a great many pieces of paper whirling about a room, they would look confused until you picked out *one* piece of paper to be *the* piece of paper by which everything else was in motion. In other words, a confusing motion can be understood by conceiving one thing to be motionless.

In a stream of traffic, all would be confusion unless you were to conceive *one* car to be motionless in relation to the other cars and so to see others in relation to the one.

The switchboard operator, receiving ten calls at once, solves the confusion by labeling–correctly or incorrectly–*one* call as the first call to receive her attention. The confusion of "ten calls all at once" becomes less confusing the moment she singles out one call to be answered.

The shop foreman, confronted by three emergencies and an accident, needs only to elect his *first* target of attention to start the cycle of bringing about order again.

Until one selects *one* datum, *one* factor, *one* particular in a confusion of particles, the confusion continues. The *one* thing selected and used becomes the *stable datum* for the remainder.

Any body of knowledge, more particularly and exactly, is built from *one datum*. That is its *stable datum*. Invalidate it and the entire body of knowledge falls apart. A stable datum does not have to be the correct one. It is simply the one that keeps things from being in a confusion and on which others are aligned.

Now, in teaching a young aspirant to use a machine, he failed to grasp your directions, if he did, because he lacked a stable datum. *One fact* had to be brought home to him first. Grasping that, he could grasp others. One is stupid, then, or confused in any confusing situation until he has fully grasped *one fact* or *one item*.

Confusions, no matter how big and formidable they may seem, are composed of data or factors or particles. They have pieces. Grasp *one* piece or locate it thoroughly. Then see how the others function in relation to it and you have steadied the confusion. And relating *other* things to what you have grasped, you will soon have mastered the confusion in its entirety.

In teaching a boy to run a machine, don't throw a torrent of data at him and then point out his errors—that's confusion to him, that makes him respond stupidly. Find some entrance point to his confusion, *one datum*. Tell him, "This is a machine." It may be that all the directions were flung at someone who had no real certainty, no real order in existence. "This is a machine," you say. Then make him sure of it. Make him feel it, fiddle with it, push at it. "This is a machine," tell him. And you'd be surprised how long it may take, but you'd be surprised as well how his certainty increases. Out of all the complexities he must learn to operate it, he must know *one datum* first. It is not even important *which* datum he first learns well, beyond that it is better to teach him a *simple basic datum*. You can show him what it does, you can explain to him the final product, you can tell him why *he* has been selected to run this machine. *But* you *must* make one basic datum clear to him or else he will be lost in confusion.

Confusion is *uncertainty*. Confusion is *stupidity*. Confusion is *insecurity*. When you think of uncertainty, stupidity and insecurity, think of confusion and you'll have it down pat.

What, then, is *certainty*? Lack of confusion. What, then, is *intelligence*? Ability to handle confusion. What, then, is *security*? The ability to go through or around or to bring order to confusion. Certainty, intelligence and security are *lack of* or *ability to handle* confusion.

How does luck fit into confusion? Luck is the hope that some uncontrolled chance will get one through. Counting on luck is an abandonment of control. That's apathy.

There is "good control" and "bad control." The difference between them is *certainty* and *uncertainty.* Good control is certain, positive, predictable. Bad control is uncertain, variable and unpredictable. With good control, one can be certain. With bad control, one is never certain.

A foreman who makes a rule effective today but not tomorrow, who makes George obey but not James, is exercising bad control. In that foreman's wake will come uncertainty and insecurity, no matter what his personal attributes may be.

Because there can be so much uncertain, stupid control, some of us begin to believe that all control is bad. But this is very far from true. Control is necessary if one would bring any order into confusions. One must be able to control things, his body, his thoughts, at least to some degree, to do anything whatever.

A confusion could be called an "uncontrolled randomness." Only those who can exert some control over that randomness can handle confusions. Those who cannot exert control actually breed confusions.

The difference between good and bad control then becomes more obvious. The difference between good and bad, here, is *degree.* A thorough, positive control can be predicted by others. Therefore it is good control. A non-positive, sloppy control cannot be predicted. Therefore it is a bad control. Intention also has something to do with control. Control can be used for constructive purposes or destructive purposes. But you will discover that when destructive purposes are *intended,* bad control is used.

Thus there is a great deal to this entire subject of *confusion*. You may find it rather odd for confusion itself to be used here as a target. But you will find that it is an excellent common denominator to all that we consider evil in life. And if one can become master of confusions, his attention is freed for *constructive* activity. So long as one is being confused by confusions, all he can think about are *destructive* things–what he wants to do *most* is to destroy the confusion.

So let us then learn first how to destroy confusions. And this we find is a rather simple thing.

When *all* particles seem to be in motion, halt one and see how the others move according to *it* and then you will find less confusion present. With *one* adopted as a *stable datum,* others can be made to fall in line. Thus an emergency, a machine, a job or life itself can be viewed and understood and one can be free.

Let us take a glance at how this works. One can handle this entire problem, as people most often do, by entering into the problem the single datum, "I can get and hold a job." By clutching to this as a single belief, the confusions and insecurities of life become less effective, less confusing.

But suppose one has done this: Without further investigating the problem, one, when young, gritted his teeth and shut his eyes and said, "I can get and hold a job, come what may. Therefore I am not going to worry about the economics of existence anymore." Well, that was fine.

Later on, without warning, one got fired. One was out of work for ten weeks. He felt then, even when he did get a new job, less secure, less confident. And let us say that some accident occurred and one was out of a job again. When once more unemployed, he was once more even less confident, less secure. Why?

Let us take a look at the opposite side of this Doctrine of the Stable Datum. If we do, we learn that confusions are held ineffective by stable data and that when the stable datum is shaken, the confusion comes into being again.

Let us envision a confusion as stopped. It is still scattered, but it is stopped. What stopped it? The adoption of a stable datum. Let us say that one was bothered badly in the home by a mother-in-law. One day, after a quarrel, one stalked out and by inspiration said to himself, "All mothers-in-law are evil."

That was a decision. That, rightly or wrongly, was a stable datum adopted in a confusion. At once one felt better. He could deal with or live with the problem now. He knew that "All mothers-in-law were evil." It wasn't true, but it was a stable datum.

Then one day, when he was in trouble, his mother-in-law stepped forward, true-blue, and paid not only the rent but the other debt too. At once he felt very confused. This act of kindness should not have been a thing to bring in confusion. After all, hadn't she solved the problem? Then why does one feel upset about it? *Because the stable datum has been shaken.* The entire confusion of the past problem came into action again by reason of the demonstrated falsity of the stable datum.

To make anyone confused, all you have to do is locate their stable data and invalidate them. By criticism or proof, it is only necessary to shake these few stable data to get all a person's confusions back into action.

You see, stable data do not have to be *true*. They are simply *adopted*. When adopted, then one looks at other data in relation to them. Thus the adoption of *any* stable datum will tend to nullify the confusion addressed. *But* if that stable datum is shaken, invalidated, disproven, then one is left again with the confusion.

Of course, all one has to do is adopt a new stable datum or put the old stable datum back in place. But he'd have to know Scientology in order to accomplish this smoothly.

Let us say one has no fears of national economy because of a heroic political figure who is trying his best. That man is the stable datum to all one's confusions about national economy. Thus one "isn't worried." But one day, circumstances or his political enemies shake him as a datum. They "prove" he was really dishonest. One then becomes worried all over again about national economy.

Maybe you adopted some philosophy because the speaker seemed such a pleasant chap. Then some person carefully proves to you that the speaker was actually a thief or worse. One adopted the philosophy because one needed some peace from his thoughts. Invalidating the speaker would then at once bring back the confusion one faced originally.

All right. We looked at the confusion of the workaday world when we were young, and we held it all back by stating grimly, "I can get and keep a job." That was the stable datum. We did get a job. But we got fired. The confusion of the workaday world then became very confusing. If we have only the one stable datum, "I can get and keep a job," as our total answer to all the various problems of work, then assuredly one is going to spend some confusing periods in his working life. A far, far better stable datum would be, "I understand about life and jobs. Therefore I can get, hold and improve them."

THE MAN WHO SUCCEEDS

SCIENTOLOGY:
A NEW SLANT ON LIFE

L. RON HUBBARD

"A workman is not just a workman.
A laborer is not just a laborer. An office
worker is not just an office worker.
They are living, breathing, important
pillars on which the entire structure of
our civilization is erected. They are
not cogs in a mighty machine.
They are the machine itself."

THE MAN WHO SUCCEEDS

THE CONDITIONS OF SUCCESS are few and easily stated.

Jobs are not held, consistently and in actuality, by flukes of fate or fortune. Those who depend upon luck generally experience bad luck.

The ability to hold a job depends, in the main, upon ability. One must be able to control his work and must be able to be controlled in doing his work. One must be able, as well, to leave certain areas uncontrolled. One's intelligence is directly related to his ability. There is no such thing as being too smart. But there is such a thing as being too stupid.

But one may be both able and intelligent without succeeding. A vital part of success is the ability to handle and control not only one's tools of the trade, but the people with whom one is surrounded. In order to do this, one must be capable of a very high level of affinity, he must be able to tolerate massive realities and he must, as well, be able to give and receive communication.

The ingredients of success are then, first, an ability to confront work with joy and not horror, a wish to do work for its own sake, not because one "has to have a paycheck." One must be able to work without driving oneself or experiencing deep depths of exhaustion. If one experiences these things, there is something wrong with him. There is some element in his environment that he should be controlling that he isn't controlling. Or his accumulated injuries are such as to make him shy away from all people and masses with whom he should be in intimate contact.

The ingredients of successful work are training and experience in the subject being addressed, good general intelligence and ability, a capability of high affinity, a tolerance of reality and the ability to communicate and receive ideas.

Given these things, there is left only a slim chance of failure. Given these things, a man can ignore all of the accidents of birth, marriage or fortune–for birth, marriage and fortune are not capable of placing these necessary ingredients in one's hands.

One could have all the money in the world and yet be unable to perform an hour's honest labor. Such a man would be a miserably unhappy one.

The person who studiously avoids work usually works far longer and far harder than the man who pleasantly confronts it and does it. Men who cannot work are not happy men.

Work is the stable datum of this society. Without something to do, there is nothing for which to live. A man who cannot work is as good as dead and usually prefers death and works to achieve it.

The mysteries of life are not today, with Scientology, very mysterious. Mystery is not a needful ingredient. Only the very aberrated man desires to have vast secrets held away from him.

Scientology has slashed through many of the complexities which have been erected for men and has bared the core of these problems. Scientology, for the first time in Man's history, can predictably raise intelligence, increase ability, bring about a return to the ability to play a game and permits Man to escape from the dwindling spiral of his own disabilities. Therefore work itself can become, again, a pleasant and happy thing.

There is one thing that has been learned in Scientology, which is very important to the state of mind of the workman. One very often feels, in his society, that he is working for the immediate paycheck and that he does not gain, for the whole society, anything of any importance. He does not know several things. One of these is how *few* good workmen are. On the level of executives, it is interesting to note how precious any large company finds a man who can handle and control jobs and men *really* is. Such people are rare. All the empty space in the structure of this workaday world is at the top.

And there is another thing which is quite important. And that is the fact that the world today has been led to believe–by mental philosophies calculated to betray it–that when one is dead, it is all over and done with and one has no further responsibility for anything. It is highly doubtful if this is true. One inherits tomorrow what he died out of yesterday.

Another thing we know is that men are not dispensable. It is a mechanism of old philosophies to tell men that "If they think they are indispensable, they should go down to the graveyard and take a look–those men were indispensable too." This is the sheerest foolishness. If you really looked carefully in the graveyard, you would find the machinist who set the models going in yesteryear and without whom there would be no industry today. It is doubtful if such a feat is being performed just now.

A workman is not just a workman. A laborer is not just a laborer. An office worker is not just an office worker. They are living, breathing, important pillars on which the entire structure of our civilization is erected. They are not cogs in a mighty machine. They are the machine itself.

We have come to a low level of the ability to work. Offices depend very often on no more than one or two men and the additional staffs seem to add only complexity to the activities of the scene. Countries move forward on the production of just a few factories. It is as though the world were being held together by a handful of desperate men who, by working themselves to death, may keep the rest of the world going.

But again, they may not.

It is to them that this is dedicated.

A TRUE GROUP

SCIENTOLOGY:
A NEW SLANT ON LIFE

L. RON HUBBARD

" Any member of the group has the right to demand the most and highest level of the ideals, rationale and ethics of the group and to demand that these be maintained. A true group owes to its individual members their livelihood and a chance for their future generations. "

A TRUE GROUP

A TRUE GROUP IS one which has ideals, ethics, rationale and a dynamic to carry forth its ideals and rationale on the ethics standard it has selected.

The first right of any true group is to survive.

All groups must have goals. Only the deterioration of the goals of the group or the reaching of all the goals of the group can bring about the decline of the group or the individuals within it. It is therefore incumbent upon any group to have a postulated set of goals which are continuing goals, to have a major goal which cannot be reached all in a breath, but also to have minor goals which go in progression toward major goals which go in progression towards super-major goals.

The group has the perfect right to demand the help, life or, in a continuing sense, the energy and devotion of any member of the group. Any member of the group has the right to demand the most and highest level of the ideals, rationale and ethics of the group and to demand that these be maintained. A true group owes to its individual members their livelihood and a chance for their future generations. The members must not deny to the group its right to expand and perpetuate itself, but must contribute fully and wholly to these.

An individual has the right to contribute to the group and the group has the right to expect every individual to contribute to it to his maximum ability and energy. The individual has the right to expect to be contributed to from the group and for the group to safeguard him insofar as is possible in the maintenance of the group and the reaching by the group of its goals.

THE CREDO OF A
TRUE GROUP MEMBER

1 The successful participant of a group is that participant who closely approximates, in his own activities, the ideal, ethic and rationale of the overall group.

2 The responsibility of the individual for the group as a whole should not be less than the responsibility of the group for the individual.

3 The group member has, as part of his responsibility, the smooth operation of the entire group.

4 A group member must exert and insist upon his rights and prerogatives as a group member and insist upon the rights and prerogatives of the group as a group and let not these rights be diminished in any way or degree for any excuse or claimed expeditiousness.

5 The member of a true group must exert and practice his right to contribute to the group. And he must insist upon the right of the group to contribute to him. He should recognize that a myriad of group failures will result when either of these contributions is denied as a right. (A welfare state being that state in which the member is not permitted to contribute to the state, but must take contribution from the state.)

6 Enturbulence of the affairs of the group by sudden shifts of plans unjustified by circumstances, breakdown of recognized channels or cessation of useful operations in a group must be refused and blocked by the member of a group. He should take care not to enturbulate a manager and thus lower ARC.

7 Failure in planning or failure to recognize goals must be corrected by the group member, for the group, by calling the matter to conference or acting upon his own initiative.

8 A group member must coordinate his initiative with the goals and rationale of the entire group and with other individual members, well publishing his activities and intentions so that all conflicts may be brought forth in advance.

9 A group member must insist upon his right to have initiative.

10 A group member must study and understand and work with the goals, rationale and executions of the group.

11 A group member must work toward becoming as expert as possible in his specialized technology and skill in the group and must assist other individuals of the group to an understanding of that technology and skill and its place in the organizational necessities of the group.

12 A group member should have a working knowledge of all technologies and skills in the group in order to understand them and their place in the organizational necessities of the group.

13 On the group member depends the height of the ARC of the group. He must insist upon high-level communication lines and clarity in affinity and reality and know the consequence of not having such conditions. *And he must work continually and actively to maintain high ARC in the organization.*

14 A group member has the right of pride in his tasks and a right of judgment and handling in those tasks.

15 A group member must recognize that he is, himself, a manager of some section of the group and/or its tasks and that he himself must have both the knowledge and right of management in that sphere for which he is responsible.

16 The group member should not permit laws to be passed which limit or proscribe the activities of all the members of the group because of the failure of some of the members of the group.

17 The group member should insist on flexible planning and unerring execution of plans.

18 The performance of duty at optimum by every member of the group should be understood by the group member to be the best safeguard of his own and the group survival. It is the pertinent business of any member of the group that optimum performance be achieved by any other member of the group, whether chain of command or similarity of activity sphere warrants such supervision or not.

THE CREDO OF A
GOOD AND SKILLED MANAGER

To be effective and successful a manager must:

1 Understand as fully as possible the goals and aims of the group he manages. He must be able to see and embrace the *ideal* attainment of the goal as envisioned by a goal maker. He must be able to tolerate and better the *practical* attainments and advances of which his group and its members may be capable. He must strive to narrow, always, the ever-existing gulf between the *ideal* and the *practical*.

2 He must realize that a primary mission is the full and honest interpretation by himself of the ideal and ethic and their goals and aims to his subordinates and the group itself. He must lead, creatively and persuasively, toward these goals his subordinates, the group itself and the individuals of the group.

3 He must embrace the organization and act solely for the entire organization and never form or favor cliques. His judgment of individuals of the group should be solely in the light of their worth to the entire group.

4 He must never falter in sacrificing individuals to the good of the group, both in planning and execution and in his justice.

5 He must protect all established communication lines and complement them where necessary.

6 He must protect all affinity in his charge and have, himself, an affinity for the group itself.

7 He must attain always to the highest creative reality.

8 His planning must accomplish, in the light of goals and aims, the activity of the entire group. He must never let organizations grow and sprawl but, learning by pilots, must keep organizational planning fresh and flexible.

9 He must recognize in himself the rationale of the group and receive and evaluate the data out of which he makes his solutions with the highest attention to the truth of that data.

10 He must constitute himself on the orders of service to the group.

11 He must permit himself to be served well as to his individual requirements, practicing an economy of his own efforts and enjoying certain comforts to the end of keeping high his rationale.

12 He should require of his subordinates that they relay into their own spheres of management the whole and entire of his true feelings and the reasons for his decisions as clearly as they can be relayed and expanded and interpreted only

for the greater understanding of the individuals governed by those subordinates.

13 He must never permit himself to pervert or mask any portion of the ideal and ethic on which the group operates, nor must he permit the ideal and ethic to grow old and outmoded and unworkable. He must never permit his planning to be perverted or censored by subordinates. He must never permit the ideal and ethic of the group's individual members to deteriorate, using always reason to interrupt such a deterioration.

14 He must have faith in the goals, faith in himself and faith in the group.

15 He must lead by demonstrating always creative and constructive subgoals. He must not drive by threat and fear.

16 He must realize that every individual in the group is engaged in some degree in the managing of other men, life and the physical universe and that a liberty of management within this code should be allowed to every such submanager.

Thus conducting himself, a manager can win empire for his group, whatever that empire may be.

L. RON HUBBARD

ON FAMILY

ON MARRIAGE

SCIENTOLOGY:
A NEW SLANT ON LIFE

L. RON HUBBARD

"Communication
is the root of marital success
from which a strong union can
grow and non-communication
is the rock on which the ship
will bash out her keel."

ON MARRIAGE

COMMUNICATION IS THE ROOT of marital success from which a strong union can grow and non-communication is the rock on which the ship will bash out her keel.

In the first place, men and women aren't too careful on "whom they up and marry." In the absence of any basic training about neurosis, psychosis or how to judge a good cook or a good wage earner, that tricky, treacherous and not always easy-to-identify thing called "love" is the sole guiding factor in the selection of mates. It is too much to expect of a society above the level of ants to be entirely practical about an institution as basically impractical as marriage. Thus it is not amazing that the mis-selection of partners goes on with such abandon.

There are ways, however, not only to select a marriage partner, but also to guarantee the continuation of that marriage, and these ways are simple. They depend, uniformly, upon communication.

There should be some parity of intellect and sanity between a husband and wife for them to have a successful marriage.

In Western culture, it is expected that the women shall have some command of the humanities and sciences. It is easy to establish the educational background of a potential marriage partner. It is not so easy to gauge their capability regarding sex, family or children, or their sanity.

In the past, efforts were made to establish sanity with inkblots, square blocks and tests with marbles to find out if anybody had lost any. The resulting figures had to be personally interpreted with a crystal ball and then reinterpreted for application.

In Scientology, there is a test for sanity and comparative sanity which is so simple that anyone can apply it: What is the "communication lag" of the individual? When asked a question, how long does it take him to answer? When a remark is addressed to him, how long does it take for him to register and return? The fast answer tells of the fast mind and the sane mind, providing the answer is a sequitur. The slow answer tells of downscale. Marital partners who have the same communication lag will get along. Where one partner is fast and one is slow, the situation will become unbearable to the fast partner and miserable to the slow one.

The repair of a marriage which is going on the rocks does not always require the processing of the marriage partners. It may be that another family factor is in the scene. This may be in the person of a relative, such as the mother-in-law. How does one solve this factor without using a shotgun? This, again, is simple. The mother-in-law, if there is trouble in the family, is responsible for cutting communication lines or diverting communication. One or the other of the partners, then, is cut off the communication channel on which he belongs. He senses this and objects strenuously to it.

Jealousy is the largest factor in breaking up marriages. Jealousy comes about because of the insecurity of the jealous person and the jealousy may or may not have foundation. This person is afraid of hidden communication lines and will do anything to try to uncover them. This acts upon the other partner to make him feel that his communication lines are being cut, for he thinks himself entitled to have open communication lines, whereas his marital partner insists that he shut many of them. The resultant rows are violent, as represented by the fact that where jealousy exists in a profession such as acting, insurance companies will not issue policies–the suicide rate is too high.

The subject of marriage could not be covered in many chapters, but here are given the basic clues to a successful marriage–Communicate!

How to Live with Children

Scientology:
A New Slant on Life

L. Ron Hubbard

" Potentially, parent, he's saner than you are and the world is a lot brighter. His sense of values and reality are sharper. Don't dull them. And your child will be a fine, tall, successful human being. "

HOW TO LIVE
WITH CHILDREN

THE ADULT IS the problem in child raising, not the child. An adult has certain rights around children which children and modern adults rather tend to ignore.

A good, stable adult with love and tolerance in his heart is about the best therapy a child can have.

The main consideration in raising children is the problem of training them without breaking them. The Jesuits had a system which is reported to have been workable, but the system perished with the Jesuits. In contradistinction, the American Medical Association–an organization devoted to efforts to control the practices of doctors–came out with a pamphlet, a masterpiece of nonsense, which was called *How to Control Your Child*. That's just what you don't want to do. You want to raise your child in such a way that you don't have to control him, so that he will be in full possession of himself at all times. Upon that depends his good behavior, his health, his sanity.

The good ex-barbers to the contrary, children are not dogs. They can't be trained like dogs are trained. They are not controllable items. They are, and let's not overlook the point, men and women. A *child* is not a special species of animal distinct from Man. A child is a man or a woman who has not attained full growth.

Any law which applies to the behavior of men and women applies to children.

How would you like to be pulled and hauled and ordered about and restrained from doing whatever you wanted to do? You'd resent it. The only reason a child "doesn't" resent it is because he's small. You'd half-murder somebody who treated you, an adult, with the orders, contradiction and disrespect given to the average child. The child doesn't strike back because he isn't big enough. He gets your floor muddy, interrupts your nap, destroys the peace of the home instead. If he had equality with you in the matter of rights, he'd not ask for this "revenge." This "revenge" is standard child behavior.

A child has a right to his self-determinism. You say that if he is not restrained from pulling things down on him, running into the road, etc., etc., he'll be hurt. What are you, as an adult, doing to make that child live in rooms or an environment where he *can* be hurt? The fault is yours, not his, if he breaks things.

The sweetness and love of a child is preserved only so long as he can exert his own self-determinism. You interrupt that and, to a degree, you interrupt his life.

There are only two reasons why a child's right to decide for himself has to be interrupted—the fragility and danger of his environment and *you*. For you work out on him the things that were done to you, regardless of what you think.

There are two courses you can take. Give the child leeway in an environment he can't hurt, which can't badly hurt him and which doesn't greatly restrict his space and time. And you can clean up your own aberrations to a point where your tolerance equals or surpasses his lack of education in how to please you.

When you give a child something, it's *his*. It's not still yours. Clothes, toys, quarters, what he has been given *must remain under his exclusive control*. So he tears up his shirt, wrecks his bed, breaks his fire engine. It's *none of your business*. How would you like to have somebody give you a Christmas present and then tell you, day after day thereafter, what you are to do with it and even punish you if you failed to care for it the way the donor thinks? You'd wreck that donor and ruin that present. You know you would. The child wrecks your nerves when you do it to him. That's revenge. He cries. He pesters you. He breaks your things. He "accidentally" spills his milk. And he wrecks the possession *on purpose* about which he is so often cautioned. Why? Because he is fighting for his own self-determinism, his own right to own and make his weight felt on his environment. This "possession" is another channel by which he can be controlled. So he has to fight the possession and the controller.

Doubtless, the worthy ex-barbers were so poorly raised they think *control* is the ne plus ultra of child raising. If you want to control your child, simply break him into complete apathy and he'll be as obedient as any hypnotized half-wit. If you want to know how to control him, get a book on dog training, name the child Rex and teach him first to "fetch" and then to "sit up" and then to bark for his food. You can train a child that way. Sure you can. But it's your hard luck if he turns out to be a bloodletter. Only don't be halfhearted about it. Simply *train* him. "Speak, Roger!" "Lie down!" "Roll over!"

Of course, you'll have a hard time of it. This—a slight medical oversight—is a *human being*. You better charge right in and do what you can to break him into apathy quick. A club is best. Tying him in a closet without food for a few days is fairly successful. The best recommended tactic, however, is simply to use a straitjacket and muffs on him until he is so docile and imbecilic that he couldn't be trained in anything but psychology for a profession. I'm warning you that it's going to be tough; it will be tough because Man became king of the beasts only because he couldn't as a species be licked. He doesn't easily go into an obedient apathy like dogs do. *Men* own *dogs* because men are self-determined and dogs aren't.

The reason people started to confuse children with dogs and to start training children with force lies in the field of psychology. The psychologist worked on "principles" as follows:

"Man is evil."

"Man must be trained into being a social animal."

"Man must adapt to his environment."

As these postulates aren't true, psychology doesn't work. And if you ever saw a wreck, it's the child of a professional psychologist. Attention to the world around us, instead of to texts somebody thought up after reading somebody's texts, shows us the fallacy of these postulates.

The reason Scientology does what it does is because Scientology is based on some workable postulates. Psychology didn't even know you had to have postulates and axioms to have a science—didn't even realize that the above constituted their basic creed. The above is formulated from an inspection of their vast tomes.

The actuality is quite opposite the previous beliefs.

The truth lies in this direction:

Man is basically good.

Only by severe aberration can Man be made evil. Severe training drives him into nonsociability.

Man must retain his personal ability to adapt his environment to him to remain sane.

A man is as sane and safe as he is self-determined.

In raising your child, you must avoid "training" him into a social animal. Your child begins by being more sociable, more dignified than you are. In a relatively short time, the treatment he gets so checks him that he revolts. This revolt can be intensified until he is a terror to have around. He will be noisy, thoughtless, careless of possessions, unclean—anything, in short, which will annoy you. Train him, control him and you'll lose his love. You've lost the child forever that you seek to control and own.

Permit a child to sit on your lap. He'll sit there, contented. Now put your arms around him and constrain him to sit there. Do this even though he wasn't even trying to leave. Instantly, he'll squirm. He'll fight to get away from you. He'll get angry. He'll cry. Recall now, he was happy before you started to hold him. You should actually make this experiment.

Your efforts to mold, train, control this child in general react on him exactly like trying to hold him on your lap.

Of course, you will have difficulty if this child of yours has already been trained, controlled, ordered about, denied his own possessions. In mid-flight, you change your tactics. You try to give him his freedom. He's so suspicious of you, he will have a terrible time trying to adjust. The transition period will be terrible.

But at the end of it, you'll have a well-ordered, well-trained, social child, thoughtful of you and, very important to you, a child who loves you.

The child who is under constraint, shepherded, handled, controlled, has a very bad anxiety postulated. His parents are survival entities. They mean food, clothing, shelter, affection. This means he wants to be near them. He wants to love them, naturally, being their child.

But on the other hand, his parents are non-survival entities. *His whole being and life depend upon his rights to use his own decision about his movements and his possessions and his body.* Parents seek to interrupt this out of the mistaken idea that a child is an idiot who won't learn unless "controlled." So he has to fight shy, to fight against, to annoy and harass an enemy.

Here is anxiety. "I love them dearly. I also need them. But they mean an interruption of my ability, my mind, my potential life. What am I going to do about my parents? I can't live with them. I can't live without them. Oh, dear, oh, dear!" There he sits in his rompers, running this problem through his head. That problem, that anxiety, will be with him for eighteen years, more or less. And it will half-wreck his life.

Freedom for the child means freedom for you.

Abandoning the possessions of the child to their fate means eventual safety for the child's possessions.

What terrible willpower is demanded of a parent not to give constant streams of directions to a child! What agony to watch his possessions going to ruin! What upset to refuse to order his time and space!

But it has to be done if you want a well, a happy, a careful, a beautiful, an intelligent child!

Another thing is the matter of contribution. You have no right to deny your child the right to contribute.

A human being feels able and competent only so long as he is permitted to contribute as much as or more than he has contributed to him.

A man can overcontribute and feel secure in an environment. He feels insecure the moment he undercontributes, which is to say, gives less than he receives. If you don't believe this, recall a time when everyone else brought something to the party, but you didn't. How did you feel?

A human being will revolt against and distrust any source which contributes to him more than he contributes to it.

Parents, naturally, contribute more to a child than the child contributes back. As soon as the child sees this, he becomes unhappy. He seeks to raise his contribution level. Failing, he gets angry at the contribution source. He begins to detest his parents. They try to override this revolt by contributing more. The child revolts more. It is a bad "dwindling spiral" because the end of it is that the child will go into apathy.

You *must* let the child contribute to you. You can't order him to contribute. You can't command him to mow the grass and then think that that's contribution. He has to figure out what his contribution is and then give it. If he hasn't selected it, it isn't his, but only more control.

A baby contributes by trying to make you smile. The baby will show off. A little older, he will dance for you, bring you sticks, try to repeat your work motions to help you. If you don't accept those smiles, those dances, those sticks, those work motions in the spirit they are given, you have begun to interrupt the child's contribution. Now he will start to get anxious. He will do unthinking and strange things to your possessions in an effort to make them "better" for you. You scold him. That finishes him.

Something else enters in here. And that is *data*. How can a child possibly know what to contribute to you or his family or home if he hasn't any idea of the working principles on which it runs?

A family is a group with the common goal of group survival and advancement. The child, not allowed to contribute or failing to understand the goals and working principles of family life, is cast adrift from the family. He is shown he is not part of the family because he can't contribute. So he becomes anti-family–the first step on the road to being anti-social. He spills milk, annoys your guests and yells outside your window in "play." He'll even get sick just to make you work. He is shown to be nothing by being shown that he isn't powerful enough to contribute.

You can do nothing more than accept the smiles, the dances, the sticks of the very young. But as soon as a child can understand, he should be given the whole story of the family operation.

What is the source of his allowance? How come there's food? Clothes? A clean house? A car?

Daddy works. He expends hours and brains and brawn and for this he gets money. The money, handed over at a store, buys food. A car is cared for because of money scarcity. A calm house and care of Daddy means Daddy works better, and that means food and clothes and cars.

Education is necessary because one earns better after he has learned.

Play is necessary in order to give a reason for hard work.

Give him the whole picture. If he's been revolting, he may keep right on revolting. But he'll eventually come around.

First of all, a child needs *security.* Part of that security is understanding. Part of it is a code of conduct which is invariable. What is against law today can't be ignored tomorrow.

You can actually punish a child to defend your rights, so long as he owns what he owns and can contribute to you and work for you.

Adults have rights. He ought to know this. A child has as his goal growing up. If an adult doesn't have more rights, why grow up? Who the devil would be an adult in this year of our Lord anyway?

The child has a duty toward you. He has to be able to take care of you. Not an illusion that he is, but actually. And you have to have patience to allow yourself to be cared for sloppily until, by sheer experience itself–not by your directions–he learns how to do it well. Care for the child–nonsense. He's probably got a better grasp of immediate situations than you have, you beaten-up adult. Only when he's almost psychotic with aberration will a child be an accident-prone.

You're well and enjoy life because you aren't *owned.* You *couldn't* enjoy life if you were shepherded and owned. You'd revolt. And if your revolt was quenched, you'd turn into a subversive. That's what you make out of your child when you own, manage and control him.

Potentially, parent, he's saner than you are and the world is a lot brighter. His sense of values and reality are sharper. Don't dull them. And your child will be a fine, tall, successful human being. Own, control, manage and reject, and you'll get the treatment you deserve–subversive revolt.

Now, are we going to have a happy house around here or aren't we?

On How to Get Along with Others

Two Rules
for Happy Living

Scientology:
A New Slant on Life

L. Ron Hubbard

" *To be happy, one only*
must be able to confront
(which is to say, experience)
those things that are. "

TWO RULES
FOR HAPPY LIVING

1. *Be able to experience anything.*

2. *Cause only those things which others are able to experience easily.*

Man has had many golden rules. The Buddhist rule of "Do unto others as you would have these others do unto you" has been repeated often in other religions. But such golden rules, while they served to advance Man above the animal, resulted in no sure sanity, success or happiness. Such a golden rule gives only the cause-point, or at best the reflexive effect-point. This is a self-done-to-self thing and tends to put all on obsessive cause. It gives no thought to what one does about the things done to one by others not so indoctrinated.

How does one handle the evil things done to him? It is not told in the Buddhist rule. Many random answers resulted. Amongst them are the answers of Christian Science (effects on self don't exist), the answers of early Christians (become a martyr), the answers of Christian ministers (condemn all sin). Such answers to effects created on one bring about a somewhat less than sane state of mind–to say nothing of unhappiness.

After one's house has burned down and the family cremated, it is no great consolation to (*a*) pretend it didn't happen, (*b*) liken oneself to Job or (*c*) condemn all arsonists.

So long as one fears or suffers from the effect of violence, one will have violence against him. When one *can* experience exactly what is being done to one, ah magic, it does not happen!

How to be happy in this universe is a problem few prophets or sages have dared contemplate directly. We find them "handling" the problem of happiness by assuring us that Man is doomed to suffering. They seek not to tell us how to be happy, but how to endure being unhappy. Such casual assumption of the impossibility of happiness has led us to ignore any real examination of ways to be happy. Thus we have floundered forward toward a negative goal–get rid of all the unhappiness on Earth and one would have a livable Earth. If one seeks to get rid of something continually, one admits continually he cannot confront it–and thus everyone went downhill. Life became a dwindling spiral of *more* things we could not confront. And thus we went toward blindness and unhappiness.

To be happy, one only must be *able* to confront (which is to say, experience) those things that are.

Unhappiness is only this: The inability to confront that which is.

Hence 1. Be able to experience anything.

The effect side of life deserves great consideration. The self-caused side also deserves examination.

To create only those effects which others could easily experience gives us a clean new rule of living. For if one does, then what might he do that he must withhold from others? There is no reason to withhold his own actions or regret them (same thing) if one's own actions are easily experienced by others.

This is a sweeping test (and definition) of good conduct – to do only those things which others can experience.

If you examine a person's life, you will find he is hung up only in those actions he did which others were not able to receive. Hence, a person's life can become a hodgepodge of violence withheld which pulls in, then, the violence others caused.

The more actions a person emanated which could not be experienced by others, the worse a person's life became. Recognizing that he was bad cause, or that there were too many bad causes already, a person ceased causing things – an unhappy state of being.

Pain, mis-emotion, unconsciousness, insanity all result from causing things others could not experience easily.

All bad acts, then, are those acts which cannot be easily experienced at the target end.

On this definition, let us review our own "bad acts." Which ones *were* bad? Only those that could not be easily experienced by another were bad. Thus, *which* of society's favorite bad acts are bad? Acts of real violence resulting in pain, unconsciousness, insanity and heavy loss could at this time be considered bad. Well, what other acts of yours do you consider "bad"? The things which you have done which you could not easily yourself experience were bad. But the things which you have done which you yourself could have experienced, had they been done to you, were *not* bad. That certainly changes one's view of things!

There is no need to lead a violent life just to prove one can experience. The idea is not to *prove* one can experience, but to regain the *ability* to experience (which can be accomplished in Scientology processing).

Thus today we have two golden rules for happiness:

1. Be able to experience anything; and

2. Cause only those things which others are able to experience easily.

Your reaction to these tells you how far you have yet to go.

And if you achieve these two golden rules, you would be one of the happiest and most successful people in this universe–for who could rule you with evil?

WHAT IS
GREATNESS?

SCIENTOLOGY:
A NEW SLANT ON LIFE

L. RON HUBBARD

" It requires real strength to love Man. And to love him despite all invitations to do otherwise, all provocations and all reasons why one should not. "

WHAT IS
GREATNESS?

THE HARDEST TASK one can have is to continue to love his fellows despite all reasons he should not.

And the true sign of sanity and greatness is to so continue.

For the one who can achieve this, there is abundant hope.

For those who cannot, there is only sorrow, hatred and despair. And these are not the things of which greatness–or sanity or happiness are made.

A primary trap is to succumb to invitations to hate.

There are those who appoint one their executioners. Sometimes, for the sake of safety of others, it is necessary to act. But it is not necessary to also hate them.

To do one's task without becoming furious at others who seek to prevent one is a mark of greatness–and sanity. And only then can one be happy.

Seeking to achieve any single desirable quality in life is a noble thing. The one most difficult – and most necessary – to achieve is to love one's fellows despite all invitations to do otherwise.

If there is any saintly quality, it is not to forgive. "Forgiveness" accepts the badness of the act. There is no reason to accept it. Further, one has to label the act as bad to forgive it. "Forgiveness" is a much lower-level action and is rather censorious.

True greatness merely refuses to change in the face of bad actions against one – and a truly great person loves his fellows because he understands them.

After all, they are all in the same trap. Some are oblivious of it, some have gone mad because of it, some act like those who betrayed them. But all, all are in the same trap – the generals, the street sweepers, the presidents, the insane. They act the way they do because they are all subject to the same cruel pressures of this universe.

Some of us are subject to those pressures and still go on doing our jobs. Others have long since succumbed and rave and torture and strut like the demented souls they are.

We can at least understand the one fact that greatness does not stem from savage wars or being known. It stems from being true to one's own decency, from going on helping others whatever they do or think or say and despite all savage acts against one, to persevere without changing one's basic attitude toward Man.

To that degree, true greatness depends on total wisdom. They act as they do because they are what they are – trapped beings, crushed beneath an intolerable burden. And if they have gone mad for it and command the devastation of whole nations in errors of explanation, still, one can understand why and can understand as well the extent of their madness. Why should one change and begin to hate just because others have lost themselves and their own destinies are too cruel for them to face?

Justice, mercy, forgiveness, all are unimportant beside the ability not to change because of provocation or demands to do so.

One must act, one must preserve order and decency. But one need not hate or seek vengeance.

It is true that beings are frail and commit wrongs. Man is basically good, but Man can act badly.

He only acts badly when his acts, done for order and the safety for others, are done with hatred. Or when his disciplines are founded only upon safety for himself regardless of all others; or worse, when he acts only out of a taste for cruelty.

To preserve no order at all is an insane act. One need only look at the possessions and environment of the insane to realize this. The able keep good order.

When cruelty in the name of discipline dominates a race, that race has been taught to hate. And that race is doomed.

The real lesson is to learn to love.

He who would walk scatheless through his days must learn this–never use what is done to one as a basis for hatred. Never desire revenge.

It requires real strength to love Man. And to love him despite all invitations to do otherwise, all provocations and all reasons why one should not.

Happiness and strength endure only in the absence of hate. To hate alone is the road to disaster. To love is the road to strength. To love in spite of all is the secret of greatness. And may very well be the greatest secret in this universe.

L. Ron Hubbard

On Human Behavior

THE ANTI-SOCIAL PERSONALITY

SCIENTOLOGY:
A NEW SLANT ON LIFE

L. RON HUBBARD

" It is important, then, to examine and list the attributes of the Anti-Social Personality. Influencing as it does the daily lives of so many, it well behooves decent people to become better informed on this subject. "

THE ANTI-SOCIAL
PERSONALITY

THERE ARE CERTAIN characteristics and mental attitudes which cause about 20 percent of a race to oppose violently any betterment activity or group.

Such people are known to have anti-social tendencies.

When the legal or political structure of a country becomes such as to favor such personalities in positions of trust, then all the civilizing organizations of the country become suppressed and a barbarism of criminality and economic duress ensues.

Crime and criminal acts are perpetrated by Anti-Social Personalities. Inmates of institutions commonly trace their state back to contact with such personalities.

Thus, in the fields of government, police activities and mental health, to name a few, we see that it is important to be able to detect and isolate this personality type so as to protect society and individuals from the destructive consequences attendant upon letting such have free rein to injure others.

As they only comprise 20 percent of the population and as only 2½ percent of this 20 percent are truly dangerous, we see that with a very small amount of effort, we could considerably better the state of society.

Well-known, even stellar examples of such a personality are, of course, Napoleon and Hitler. Dillinger, Pretty Boy Floyd, Christie and other famous criminals were well-known examples of the Anti-Social Personality. But with such a cast of characters in history, we neglect the less stellar examples and do not perceive that such personalities exist in current life, very common, often undetected.

When we trace the cause of a failing business, we will inevitably discover somewhere in its ranks the Anti-Social Personality hard at work.

In families which are breaking up, we commonly find one or the other of the persons involved to have such a personality.

Where life has become rough and is failing, a careful review of the area by a trained observer will detect one or more such personalities at work.

As there are 80 percent of us trying to get along and only 20 percent trying to prevent us, our lives would be much easier to live were we well informed as to the exact manifestations of such a personality. Thus we could detect it and save ourselves much failure and heartbreak.

It is important, then, to examine and list the attributes of the Anti-Social Personality. Influencing as it does the daily lives of so many, it well behooves decent people to become better informed on this subject.

ATTRIBUTES

The Anti-Social Personality has the following attributes:

1. He or she speaks only in very broad generalities. *"They say…"* "Everybody thinks…" "Everyone knows…" and such expressions are in continual use, particularly when imparting rumor. When asked *"Who* is everybody…" it normally turns out to be one source and from this source the Anti-Social Person has manufactured what he or she pretends is the whole opinion of the whole society.

   This is natural to them since to them all society is a large hostile generality, against the Anti-Social in particular.

2. Such a person deals mainly in bad news, critical or hostile remarks, invalidation and general suppression.

   "Gossip" or "harbinger of evil tidings" or "rumormonger" once described such persons.

   It is notable that there is no good news or complimentary remark passed on by such a person.

3. The Anti-Social Personality alters, to worsen, communication when he or she relays a message or news. Good news is stopped and only bad news, often embellished, is passed along.

   Such a person also pretends to pass on "bad news" which is in actual fact invented.

4. A characteristic, and one of the sad things about an Anti-Social Personality, is that it does not respond to treatment or reform or psychotherapy.

5. Surrounding such a personality, we find cowed or ill associates or friends who, when not driven actually insane, are yet behaving in a crippled manner in life, failing, not succeeding.

Such people make trouble for others.

When treated or educated, the near associate of the Anti-Social Personality has no stability of gain, but promptly relapses or loses his advantages of knowledge, being under the suppressive influence of the other.

Physically treated, such associates commonly do not recover in the expected time, but worsen and have poor convalescences.

It is quite useless to treat or help or train such persons so long as they remain under the influence of the anti-social connection.

The largest number of insane are insane because of such anti-social connections and do not recover easily for the same reason.

Unjustly, we seldom see the Anti-Social Personality actually in an institution. Only his "friends" and family are there.

6. The Anti-Social Personality selects habitually the wrong target.

If a tire is flat from driving over nails, he or she curses a companion or a non-causative source of the trouble. If the radio next door is too loud, he or she kicks the cat.

If A is the obvious cause, the Anti-Social Personality inevitably blames B or C or D.

7. The Anti-Social cannot finish a cycle-of-action.

Such become surrounded with incomplete projects.

8. Many Anti-Social Persons will freely confess to the most alarming crimes when forced to do so, but will have no faintest sense of responsibility for them.

Their actions have little or nothing to do with their own volition. Things "just happened."

They have no sense of correct causation and particularly cannot feel any sense of remorse or shame therefore.

9. The Anti-Social Personality supports only destructive groups and rages against and attacks any constructive or betterment group.

10. This type of personality approves only of destructive actions and fights against constructive or helpful actions or activities.

    The artist in particular is often found as a magnet for persons with anti-social personalities who see in his art something which must be destroyed and covertly, "as a friend," proceed to try.

11. Helping others is an activity which drives the Anti-Social Personality nearly berserk. Activities, however, which destroy in the name of help are closely supported.

12. The Anti-Social Personality has a bad sense of property and conceives that the idea that anyone owns anything is a pretense, made up to fool people. Nothing is ever really owned.

THE BASIC REASON

The basic reason the Anti-Social Personality behaves as he or she does lies in a hidden terror of others.

To such a person, every other being is an enemy, an enemy to be covertly or overtly destroyed.

The fixation is that survival itself depends on "keeping others down" or "keeping people ignorant."

If anyone were to promise to make others stronger or brighter, the Anti-Social Personality suffers the utmost agony of personal danger.

They reason that if they are in this much trouble with people around them weak or stupid, they would perish should anyone become strong or bright.

Such a person has no trust to a point of terror. This is usually masked and unrevealed.

When such a personality goes insane, the world is full of Martians or the FBI and each person met is really a Martian or FBI agent.

But the bulk of such people exhibit no outward signs of insanity. They appear quite rational. They can be *very* convincing.

However, the list given above consists of things which such a personality cannot detect in himself or herself. This is so true that if you thought you found yourself in one of the above, you most certainly are not anti-social. Self-criticism is a luxury the Anti-Social cannot afford. They must be *right* because they are in continual danger in their own estimation. If you proved one *wrong,* you might even send him or her into a severe illness.

Only the sane, well-balanced person tries to correct his conduct.

RELIEF

If you were to weed out of your past those Anti-Social Persons you have known and if you then disconnected, you might experience great relief.

Similarly, if society were to recognize this personality type as a sick being as they now isolate people with smallpox, both social and economic recoveries could occur.

Things are not likely to get much better so long as 20 percent of the population is permitted to dominate and injure the lives and enterprise of the remaining 80 percent.

As majority rule is the political manner of the day, so should majority sanity express itself in our daily lives without the interference and destruction of the socially unwell.

The pity of it is, they will not permit themselves to be helped and would not respond to treatment if help were attempted.

An understanding and ability to recognize such personalities could bring a major change in society and our lives.

THE SOCIAL PERSONALITY

SCIENTOLOGY:
A NEW SLANT ON LIFE

L. RON HUBBARD

" As the society runs, prospers and lives solely through the efforts of Social Personalities, one must know them as they, not the Anti-Social, are the worthwhile people. These are the people who must have rights and freedom. Attention is given to the Anti-Social solely to protect and assist the Social Personalities in the society. "

THE SOCIAL PERSONALITY

 MAN, IN HIS ANXIETIES, is prone to witch hunts.

All one has to do is designate "people wearing black caps" as the villains and one can start a slaughter of people in black caps.

This characteristic makes it very easy for the Anti-Social Personality to bring about a chaotic or dangerous environment.

Man is not naturally brave or calm in his human state. And he is not necessarily villainous.

Even the Anti-Social Personality, in his warped way, is quite certain that he is acting for the best and commonly sees himself as the only good person around, doing all for the good of everyone–the only flaw in his reasoning being that if one kills everyone else, none are left to be protected from the imagined evils. His *conduct* in his environment and toward his fellows is the only method of detecting either the Anti-Social or the Social Personalities. Their motives for self are similar–self-preservation and survival. They simply go about achieving these in different ways.

Thus, as Man is naturally neither calm nor brave, anyone to some degree tends to be alert to dangerous persons and hence, witch hunts can begin.

It is therefore even more important to identify the Social Personality than the Anti-Social Personality. One then avoids "shooting" the innocent out of mere prejudice or dislike or because of some momentary misconduct.

The Social Personality can be defined most easily by comparison with his opposite, the Anti-Social Personality.

This differentiation is easily done and no test should ever be constructed which isolates only the Anti-Social. On the same test must appear the upper as well as lower ranges of Man's actions.

A test that declares only Anti-Social Personalities without also being able to identify the Social Personality would be itself a suppressive test. It would be like answering "Yes" or "No" to the question "Do you still beat your wife?" Anyone who took it could be found guilty. While this mechanism might have suited the times of the Inquisition, it would not suit modern needs.

As the society runs, prospers and lives *solely* through the efforts of Social Personalities, one must know them as *they,* not the Anti-Social, are the worthwhile people. These are the people who must have rights and freedom. Attention is given to the Anti-Social solely to protect and assist the Social Personalities in the society.

All majority rules, civilizing intentions and even the human race will fail unless one can identify and thwart the Anti-Social Personalities and help and forward the Social Personalities in the society. For the very word "society" implies social conduct and without it there is no society at all, only a barbarism with all men, good or bad, at risk.

The frailty of showing how the harmful people can be known is that these then apply the characteristics to decent people to get them hunted down and eradicated.

The swan song of every great civilization is the tune played by arrows, axes or bullets used by the Anti-Social to slay the last decent men.

Government is only dangerous when it can be employed by and for Anti-Social Personalities. The end result is the eradication of all Social Personalities and the resultant collapse of Egypt, Babylon, Rome, Russia or the West.

You will note in the characteristics of the Anti-Social Personality that intelligence is not a clue to the Anti-Social. They are bright or stupid or average. Thus those who are extremely intelligent can rise to considerable, even head-of-state heights.

Importance and ability or wish to rise above others are likewise not indexes to the Anti-Social. When they do become important or rise, they are, however, rather visible by the broad consequences of their acts. But they are as likely to be unimportant people or hold very lowly stations and wish for nothing better.

Thus it is the twelve given characteristics alone which identify the Anti-Social Personality. And these same twelve, reversed, are the sole criteria of the Social Personality, if one wishes to be truthful about them.

The identification or labeling of an Anti-Social Personality cannot be done honestly and accurately unless one *also,* in the same examination of the person, reviews the positive side of his life.

All persons under stress can react with momentary flashes of anti-social conduct. This does not make them Anti-Social Personalities.

The true Anti-Social Person has a majority of anti-social characteristics.

The Social Personality has a majority of social characteristics.

Thus one must examine the good with the bad before one can truly label the Anti-Social or the Social.

In reviewing such matters, very broad testimony and evidence are best. One or two isolated instances determine nothing. One should search all twelve social and all twelve anti-social characteristics and decide on the basis of actual evidence, not opinion.

The twelve primary characteristics of the Social Personality are as follows:

1. The Social Personality is specific in relating circumstances. "Joe Jones said…" "The *Star* newspaper reported…" and gives sources of data where important or possible.

   He may use the generality of "they" or "people," but seldom in connection with attributing statements or opinions of an alarming nature.

2. The Social Personality is eager to relay good news and reluctant to relay bad.

   He may not even bother to pass along criticism when it doesn't matter.

   He is more interested in making another feel liked or wanted than disliked by others and tends to err toward reassurance rather than toward criticism.

3. A Social Personality passes communication without much alteration and, if deleting anything, tends to delete injurious matters.

He does not like to hurt people's feelings. He sometimes errs in holding back bad news or orders which seem critical or harsh.

4. Treatment, reform and psychotherapy, particularly of a mild nature, work very well on the Social Personality.

Whereas Anti-Social People sometimes promise to reform, they do not. Only the Social Personality can change or improve easily.

It is often enough to point out unwanted conduct to a Social Personality to completely alter it for the better.

Criminal codes and violent punishment are not needed to regulate Social Personalities.

5. The friends and associates of a Social Personality tend to be well, happy and of good morale.

A truly Social Personality quite often produces betterment in health or fortune by his mere presence on the scene.

At the very least he does not reduce the existing levels of health or morale in his associates.

When ill, the Social Personality heals or recovers in an expected manner, and is found open to successful treatment.

6. The Social Personality tends to select correct targets for correction.

He fixes the tire that is flat rather than attack the windscreen.

In the mechanical arts, he can therefore repair things and make them work.

7. Cycles-of-action begun are ordinarily completed by the Social Personality, if possible.

8. The Social Personality is ashamed of his misdeeds and reluctant to confess them. He takes responsibility for his errors.

9. The Social Personality supports constructive groups and tends to protest or resist destructive groups.

10. Destructive actions are protested by the Social Personality. He assists constructive or helpful actions.

11. The Social Personality helps others and actively resists acts which harm others.

12. Property is property of someone to the Social Personality and its theft or misuse is prevented or frowned upon.

THE BASIC MOTIVATION

The Social Personality naturally operates on the basis of the greatest good.

He is not haunted by imagined enemies, but he does recognize real enemies when they exist.

The Social Personality wants to survive and wants others to survive, whereas the Anti-Social Personality really and covertly wants others to succumb.

Basically the Social Personality wants others to be happy and do well, whereas the Anti-Social Personality is very clever in making others do very badly indeed.

A basic clue to the Social Personality is not really his successes, but his motivations. The Social Personality when successful is often a target for the Anti-Social and by this reason he may fail. But his intentions included others in his success, whereas the Anti-Social only appreciate the doom of others.

Unless we can detect the Social Personality and hold him safe from undue restraint and detect also the Anti-Social and restrain him, our society will go on suffering from insanity, criminality and war, and Man and civilization will not endure.

Of all our technical skills, such differentiation ranks the highest since, failing, no other skill can continue as the base on which it operates, civilization, will not be here to continue it.

Do not smash the Social Personality–and do not fail to render powerless the Anti-Social in their efforts to harm the rest of us.

Just because a man rises above his fellows or takes an important post does not make him an Anti-Social Personality. Just because a man can control or dominate others does not make him an Anti-Social Personality.

It is his motives in doing so and the consequences of his acts which distinguish the Anti-Social from the Social.

Unless we realize and apply the true characteristics of the two types of personality, we will continue to live in a quandary of who our enemies are and, in doing so, victimize our friends.

All men have committed acts of violence or omission for which they could be censured. In all Mankind there is not one single perfect human being.

But there are those who try to do right and those who specialize in wrong and upon these facts and characteristics you can know them.

THE THIRD PARTY LAW

SCIENTOLOGY:
A NEW SLANT ON LIFE

L. RON HUBBARD

" There are no conflicts
which cannot be resolved unless
the true promoters of them
remain hidden. "

THE THIRD PARTY LAW

I HAVE FOR A VERY long time studied the causes of violence and conflict amongst individuals and nations.

If Chaldea could vanish, if Babylon could turn to dust, if Egypt could become a badlands, if Sicily could have 160 prosperous cities and be a looted ruin before the year zero and a near desert ever since–and all this in *spite* of all the work and wisdom and good wishes and intent of human beings, then it must follow as the dark follows sunset that something must be unknown to Man concerning all his works and ways. And that this something must be so deadly and so pervasive as to destroy all his ambitions and his chances long before their time.

Such a thing would have to be some natural law unguessed at by himself.

And there *is* such a law, apparently, that answers these conditions of being deadly, unknown and embracing all activities.

The law would seem to be:

A THIRD PARTY MUST BE PRESENT AND UNKNOWN IN EVERY QUARREL FOR A CONFLICT TO EXIST.

Or

FOR A QUARREL TO OCCUR, AN UNKNOWN THIRD PARTY MUST BE ACTIVE IN PRODUCING IT BETWEEN TWO POTENTIAL OPPONENTS.

Or

WHILE IT IS COMMONLY BELIEVED TO TAKE TWO TO MAKE A FIGHT, A THIRD PARTY MUST EXIST AND MUST DEVELOP IT FOR ACTUAL CONFLICT TO OCCUR.

It is very easy to see that two in conflict are fighting. They are very visible. What is harder to see or suspect is that a Third Party existed and actively promoted the quarrel.

The usually unsuspected and "reasonable" Third Party, the bystander who denies any part of it, *is* the one that brought the conflict into existence in the first place.

The hidden Third Party, seeming at times to be a supporter of only one side, is to be found as the instigator.

This is a useful law in many aspects of life.

It *is* the cause of war.

One sees two fellows shouting bad names at each other, sees them come to blows. No one else is around. So *they,* of course, "caused the fight." But there *was* a Third Party.

Tracing these down, one comes upon incredible data. That is the trouble. The incredible is too easily rejected. One way to hide things is to make them incredible.

Clerk A and Messenger B have been arguing. They blaze into direct conflict. Each blames the other. *Neither one is correct and so the quarrel does not resolve since its true cause is not established.*

One looks into such a case *thoroughly.* He finds the incredible. The wife of Clerk A has been sleeping with Messenger B and complaining alike to both about the other.

Farmer J and Rancher K have been tearing each other to pieces for years in continual conflict. There are obvious, logical reasons for the fight. Yet it continues and does not resolve. A close search finds Banker L who, due to their losses in the fighting, is able to loan each side money, while keeping the quarrel going, and who will get their lands completely if both lose.

It goes larger. The revolutionary forces and the Russian government were in conflict in 1917. The reasons are so many the attention easily sticks on them. But only when Germany's official state papers were captured in World War II was it revealed that *Germany* had promoted the revolt and financed Lenin to spark it off, even sending him into Russia in a blacked-out train!

One looks over "personal" quarrels, group conflicts, national battles and one finds, if he searches, the Third Party, unsuspected by both combatants or, if suspected at all, brushed off as "fantastic." Yet careful documentation finally affirms it.

———

This datum is fabulously useful.

In marital quarrels, the *correct* approach of anyone counseling is to get both parties to carefully search out the *Third* Party. They may come to many *reasons* at first. These *reasons* are not *beings*. One is looking for a Third *Party,* an actual *being*. When both find the Third Party and establish proof, that will be the end of the quarrel.

Sometimes two parties, quarreling, suddenly decide to elect a being to blame. This stops the quarrel. Sometimes it is not the right being and more quarrels thereafter occur.

Two nations at each other's throats should each seek conference with the other to sift out and locate the actual Third Party. They will always find one if they look, and they *can* find the right one. As it will be found to exist in fact.

––––––––––

There are probably many technical approaches one could develop and outline in this matter.

There are many odd phenomena connected with it. An accurately spotted Third Party is usually not fought at all by either party, but only shunned.

Marital conflicts are common. Marriages can be saved by both parties really sorting out *who* caused the conflicts. There may have been (in the whole history of the marriage) several, but only one at a time.

Quarrels between an individual and an organization are nearly always caused by an individual Third Party or a third group. The organization and the individual should get together and isolate the Third Party by displaying to each other all the data they each have been fed.

Rioters and governments alike could be brought back to agreement could one get representatives of both to give each other what they have been told by *whom*.

Such conferences have tended to deal only in recriminations or conditions or abuses. They must deal in beings only, in order to succeed.

This theory might be thought to assert also that there are no bad conditions that cause conflict. There are. But these are usually *remedial by conference unless a Third Party is promoting conflict.*

In history we have a very foul opinion of the past because it is related by recriminations of two opponents and has not spotted the Third Party.

"Underlying causes" of war should read "hidden promoters."

There are no conflicts which cannot be resolved unless the true promoters of them remain hidden.

This is the natural law the ancients and moderns alike did not know.

And not knowing it, being led off into "reasons," whole civilizations have died.

It is worth knowing.

It is worth working with in any situation where one is trying to bring peace.

L. Ron Hubbard

On Honesty and Ethics

Honest People
Have Rights, Too

Scientology:
A New Slant on Life

L. Ron Hubbard

" On the day when we can

fully trust each other,

there will be peace on Earth. "

HONEST PEOPLE
HAVE RIGHTS, TOO

AFTER YOU HAVE achieved a high level of ability you will be the first to insist upon your rights to live with honest people.

When you know the technology of the mind, you know that it is a mistake to use "individual rights" and "freedom" as arguments to protect those who would only destroy.

Individual rights were not originated to protect criminals, but to bring freedom to honest men. Into this area of protection then dived those who needed "freedom" and "individual liberty" to cover their own questionable activities.

Freedom is for honest people. No man who is not himself honest can be free–he is his own trap. When his own deeds cannot be disclosed then he is a prisoner; he must withhold himself from his fellows and is a slave to his own conscience. Freedom must be deserved before any freedom is possible.

To protect dishonest people is to condemn them to their own hells. By making "individual rights" a synonym for "protect the criminal" one helps bring about a slave state for all; for where "individual liberty" is abused, an impatience with it arises which at length sweeps us all away. The targets of all disciplinary laws are the few who err. Such laws unfortunately also injure and restrict those who do not err. If all were honest, there would be no disciplinary threats.

There is only one way out for a dishonest person–facing up to his own responsibilities in the society and putting himself back into communication with his fellow man, his family, the world at large. By seeking to invoke his "individual rights" to protect himself from an examination of his deeds, he reduces just that much the future of individual liberty–for he himself is not free. Yet he infects others who are honest by using *their* right to freedom to protect himself.

Uneasy lies the head that wears a guilty conscience. And it will lie no more easily by seeking to protect misdeeds by pleas of "freedom means that you must never look at me." The right of a person to survive is directly related to his honesty.

Freedom for Man does not mean freedom to injure Man. Freedom of speech does not mean freedom to harm by lies.

Man cannot be free while there are those amongst him who are slaves to their own terrors.

The mission of a techno-space society is to subordinate the individual and control him by economic and political duress. The only casualty in a machine age is the individual and his freedom.

To preserve that freedom, one must not permit men to hide their evil intentions under the protection of that freedom. To be free, a man must be honest with himself and with his fellows. If a man uses his own honesty to protest the unmasking of dishonesty, then that man is an enemy of his own freedom.

We can stand in the sun only so long as we do not let the deeds of others bring the darkness.

Freedom is for honest men. Individual liberty exists only for those who have the ability to be free.

Today, in Scientology, we know the jailer–the person himself. And we can restore the right to stand in the sun by eradicating the evil men do to themselves.

Who would punish when he could salvage? Only a madman would break a wanted object when he could repair it–and we are not mad.

The individual must not die in this machine age–rights or no rights. The criminal and madman must not triumph with their newfound tools of destruction.

The least free person is the person who cannot reveal his own acts and who protests the revelation of the improper acts of others. On such people will be built a future political slavery where we all have numbers–and our guilt–unless we act.

It is fascinating that blackmail and punishment are the keynotes of all dark operations. What would happen if these two commodities no longer existed? What would happen if all men were free enough to speak? Then and only then would you have freedom.

On the day when we can fully trust each other, there will be peace on Earth.

ETHICS, JUSTICE AND THE DYNAMICS

SCIENTOLOGY:
A NEW SLANT ON LIFE

L. RON HUBBARD

*" If Man only knew
the simple technology of Ethics,
he could achieve for himself
the self-respect,
personal satisfaction and
success that he only believes
himself capable of dreaming of,
not attaining. "*

ETHICS, JUSTICE AND THE DYNAMICS

EVERY BEING HAS an infinite ability to survive. How well he accomplishes this is dependent on how well he uses ethics on his dynamics.*

Ethics Technology exists for the individual.

It exists to give the individual a way to increase his survival and thus free himself from the dwindling spiral of the current culture.

ETHICS

The whole subject of ethics is one which, with the society in its current state, has become almost lost.

Ethics actually consists of rationality toward the highest level of survival for the individual, the future race, the group, Mankind and the other dynamics taken up collectively.

Ethics are reason.

Man's greatest weapon is his reason.

*See *The Eight Dynamics* in this book.

The highest ethic level would be long-term survival concepts with minimal destruction, along all of the dynamics.

An optimum solution to any problem would be that solution which brought the greatest benefits to the greatest number of dynamics. The poorest solution would be that solution which brought the greatest harm to the most number of dynamics.

Activities which brought minimal survival to a lesser number of dynamics and damaged the survival of a greater number of dynamics could not be considered rational activities.

One of the reasons that this society is dying and so forth, is that it's gone too far out-ethics. Reasonable conduct and optimum solutions have ceased to be used to such an extent that the society is on the way out.

By *out-ethics* we mean an action or situation in which an individual is involved, or something the individual does, which is contrary to the ideals, best interests and survival of his dynamics.

For a man to develop a weapon capable of destroying all life on this planet (as has been done with atomic weapons and certain drugs designed by the military) and place it in the hands of the criminally insane politicians is obviously not a survival act.

For the government to actively invite and create inflation to a point where a depression is a real threat to the individuals of this society is a non-survival action to say the least.

This gets so batty that in one of the South Pacific societies, infanticide became a ruling passion. There was a limited supply of food and they wanted to keep down the birthrate. They began using abortion and if this didn't work, they killed the children. Their Second Dynamic folded up. That society has almost disappeared.

These are acts calculated to be destructive and harmful to the survival of the people of the society.

Ethics are the actions an individual takes on himself in order to accomplish optimum survival for himself and others on all dynamics. Ethical actions are survival actions. Without a use of ethics we will not survive.

We know that the Dynamic Principle of Existence is SURVIVE!

At first glance that may seem too basic. It may seem too simple. When one thinks of survival, one is apt to make the error of thinking in terms of "barest necessity." That is not survival. Survival is a graduated scale, with infinity or immortality at the top and death and pain at the bottom.

GOOD AND EVIL, RIGHT AND WRONG

Years ago I discovered and proved that Man is basically good. This means that the basic personality and the basic intentions of the individual, toward himself and others, are good.

When a person finds himself committing too many harmful acts against the dynamics, he becomes his own executioner. This gives us the proof that Man is basically good. When he finds himself committing too many evils, then, causatively, unconsciously or unwittingly, Man puts ethics in on himself by destroying himself and he does himself in without assistance from anybody else.

This is why the criminal leaves clues on the scene, why people develop strange incapacitating illnesses and why they cause themselves accidents and even decide to have an accident. When they violate their own ethics, they begin to decay. They do this all on their own, without anybody else doing anything.

The criminal who leaves clues behind is doing so in hopes that someone will come along to stop him from continuing to harm others. He is *basically* good and does not want to harm others. And in the absence of an ability to stop himself outright, he attempts to put ethics in on himself by getting thrown in prison where he will no longer be able to commit crimes.

Similarly, the person who incapacitates himself with illness or gets himself in an accident is putting ethics in on himself by lessening his ability to harm and maybe even by totally removing himself from the environment that he has been harming. When he has evil intentions, when he is being "intentionally evil," he still has an urge to also stop himself. He seeks to suppress them and when he cannot do so directly, he does so indirectly. Evil, illness and decay often go hand in hand.

Man is basically good. He is basically well intentioned. He does not want to harm himself or others. When an individual does harm the dynamics, he will destroy himself in an effort to save those dynamics. This can be proven and has been proven in innumerable cases. It is this fact which evidences that Man is basically good.

On this basis we have the concepts of right and wrong.

When we speak of ethics, we are talking about right and wrong conduct. We are talking about good and evil.

Good can be considered to be any constructive survival action. It happens that no construction can take place without some small destruction, just as the tenement must be torn down to make room for the new apartment building.

To be good, something must contribute to the individual, to his family, his children, his group, Mankind or life. To be good, a thing must contain construction which outweighs the destruction it contains. A new cure which saves a hundred lives and kills one is an acceptable cure.

Good is survival. Good is being more right than one is wrong. Good is being more successful than one is unsuccessful, along constructive lines.

Things are good which complement the survival of the individual, his family, children, group, Mankind, life and MEST.

Acts are good which are more beneficial than destructive along these dynamics.

Evil is the opposite of good, and is anything which is destructive more than it is constructive along any of the various dynamics. A thing which does more destruction than construction is evil from the viewpoint of the individual, the future race, group, species, life or MEST that it destroys.

When an act is more destructive than constructive, it is evil. It is out-ethics. When an act assists succumbing more than it assists survival, it is an evil act in the proportion that it destroys.

Good, bluntly, is survival. Ethical conduct is survival. Evil conduct is non-survival. Construction is good when it promotes survival. Construction is evil when it inhibits survival. Destruction is good when it enhances survival.

An act or conclusion is as right as it promotes the survival of the individual, future race, group, Mankind or life making the conclusion. To be entirely right would be to survive to infinity.

An act or conclusion is wrong to the degree that it is non-survival to the individual, future race, group, species or life responsible for doing the act or making the conclusion. The most wrong a person can be on the First Dynamic is dead.

The individual or group which is, on the average, more right than wrong (since these terms are not absolutes, by far) should survive. An individual who, on the average, is more wrong than right will succumb.

While there could be no absolute right or absolute wrong, a right action would depend upon its assisting the survival of the dynamics immediately concerned, a wrong action would impede the survival of the dynamics concerned.

Let us look at how these concepts of right and wrong fit into our current society.

This is a dying society. Ethics have gone so far out and are so little understood that this culture is headed for succumb at a dangerous rate.

A person is not going to come alive, this society is not going to survive, unless Ethics Technology is gotten hold of and applied.

When we look at inflation, the oil crisis, corruption of government, war, crime, insanity, drugs, sexual promiscuity, etc., we are looking at a culture on the way out. This is a direct result of individuals failing to apply ethics to their dynamics.

It actually starts with individual ethics.

Dishonest conduct is non-survival. Anything is unreasonable or evil which brings about the destruction of individuals, groups or inhibits the future of the race.

The keeping of one's word, when it has been sacredly pledged, is an act of survival, since one is then trusted, but only so long as he keeps his word.

To the weak, to the cowardly, to the reprehensibly irrational, dishonesty and underhanded dealings, the harming of others and the blighting of their hopes seem to be the only way of conducting life.

Unethical conduct is actually the conduct of destruction and fear. Lies are told because one is afraid of the consequences should one tell the truth. Destructive acts are usually done out of fear. Thus, the liar is inevitably a coward and the coward inevitably a liar.

The sexually promiscuous woman, the man who breaks faith with his friend, the covetous pervert are all dealing in such non-survival terms that degradation and unhappiness are part and parcel of their existence.

It probably seems quite normal and perfectly all right to some, to live in a highly degraded society full of criminals, drugs, war and insanity, where we are in constant threat of the total annihilation of life on this planet.

Well, let me say that this is not normal and it is not necessary. It *is* possible for individuals to lead happy productive lives without having to worry about whether or not they are going to be robbed if they walk outside their door or whether Russia is going to declare war on the United States. It is a matter of ethics. It is simply a matter of individuals applying ethics to their lives and having their dynamics in communication and surviving.

MORALS

Now we have ethics as survival. But what of such things as morals, ideals, love? Don't these things go above "mere survival"? No, they do not.

Romantic novels and television teach us that the hero always wins and that good always triumphs. But it appears that the hero doesn't always win and that good does not always triumph.

On a shorter view we can see villainy triumphing all about us. The truth of the matter is that the villainy is sooner or later going to lose. One cannot go through life victimizing one's fellow beings and wind up anything but trapped—the victim himself.

However, one doesn't observe this in the common course of life. One sees the villains succeeding everywhere, evidently amassing money, cutting their brother's throat, receiving the fruits of the courts and coming to rule over men.

Without looking at the final consequence of this, which is there just as certainly as the sun rises and sets, one begins to believe that evil triumphs whereas one has been taught that only good triumphs. This can cause the person himself to have a failure and can actually cause his downfall.

As for ideals, as for honesty, as for one's love of one's fellow man, one cannot find good survival for one or for many where these things are absent.

The criminal does not survive well. The average criminal spends the majority of his adult years caged like some wild beast and guarded from escape by the guns of good marksmen.

A man who is known to be honest is awarded survival—good jobs, good friends. And the man who has his ideals, no matter how thoroughly he may be persuaded to desert them, survives well only so long as he is true to those ideals.

Have you ever seen a doctor who, for the sake of personal gain, begins to secretly attend criminals or peddle dope? That doctor does not survive long after his ideals are laid aside.

Ideals, morals, ethics, all fall within this understanding of survival. One survives so long as he is true to himself, his family, his friends, the laws of the universe. When he fails in any respect, his survival is cut down.

In the modern dictionary, we find that *ethics* are defined as "morals" and *morals* are defined as "ethics." These two words are *not* interchangeable.

Morals should be defined as a code of good conduct laid down out of the experience of the race to serve as a uniform yardstick for the conduct of individuals and groups.

Morals are actually laws.

The origin of a moral code comes about when it is discovered through actual experience that some act is more non-survival than pro-survival. The prohibition of this act then enters into the customs of the people and may eventually become a law.

In the absence of extended reasoning powers, moral codes, so long as they provide better survival for their group, are a vital and necessary part of any culture.

Morals, however, become burdensome and protested against when they become outmoded. And although a revolt against morals may have as its stated target the fact that the code no longer is as applicable as it once was, revolts against moral codes generally occur because individuals of the group or the group itself has gone out-ethics to a point where it wishes to practice license against these moral codes, not because the codes themselves are unreasonable.

If a moral code were thoroughly reasonable, it could, at the same time, be considered thoroughly ethical. But only at this highest level could the two be called the same.

The ultimate in reason is the ultimate in survival.

Ethical conduct includes the adherence to the moral codes of the society in which we live.

JUSTICE

When an individual fails to apply ethics to himself and fails to follow the morals of the group, justice enters in.

It is not realized generally that the criminal is not only anti-social but is also anti-self.

A person who is out-ethics, who has his dynamics out of communication, is a potential or active criminal, in that crimes against the pro-survival actions of others are continually perpetrated. *Crime* might be defined as the reduction of the survival level along any one of the eight dynamics.

Justice is used when the individual's own out-ethics and destructive behavior begin to impinge too heavily on others.

In a society run by criminals and controlled by incompetent police, the citizens reactively identify any justice action or symbol with oppression.

But we have a society full of people who do not apply ethics to themselves, and in the absence of true ethics one cannot live with others and life becomes miserable. Therefore we have justice, which was developed to protect the innocent and decent.

When an individual fails to apply ethics to himself and follow the moral codes, the society takes justice action against him.

Justice, although it unfortunately cannot be trusted in the hands of Man, has as its basic intention and purpose the survival and welfare of those it serves. Justice, however, would not be needed when you have individuals who are sufficiently sane and in-ethics that they do not attempt to blunt others' survival.

Justice would be used until a person's own ethics render him fit company for his fellows.

ETHICS, JUSTICE AND YOUR SURVIVAL

In the past, the subject of ethics has not really been mentioned very much. Justice was, however. Justice systems have long been used as a substitute for ethics systems. But when you try to substitute ethics for justice, you get into trouble.

Man has not had an actual workable way of applying ethics to himself. The subjects of ethics and justice have been terribly aberrated.

We now have the technology of Ethics and Justice straightened out. This is the only road out on the subject that Man has.

People have been trying to put ethics in on themselves for eons without knowing how. Ethics evolved with the individual's attempts at continued survival.

When a person does something which is out-ethics (harms his and others' survival), he tries to right this wrong. Usually he just winds up caving himself in. (*Caved in* means mental and/or physical collapse to the extent that the individual cannot function causatively.)

They cave themselves in because, in an effort to restrain themselves and stop themselves from committing more harmful acts, they start withdrawing and withholding themselves from the area they have harmed. A person who does this becomes less and less able to influence his dynamics and thus becomes a victim of them.

It is noted here that one must have done to other dynamics those things which other dynamics now seem to have the power to do to him. Therefore he is in a position to be injured and he loses control. He can become, in fact, a zero of influence and a vacuum for trouble.

This comes about because the person does not have the basic technology of Ethics. It has never been explained to him. No one ever told him how he could get out of the hole he's gotten himself into. This technology has remained utterly unknown.

So he has gone down the chute.

Ethics is one of the primary tools a person uses to dig himself out with.

Whether he knows how to or not, every person will try to dig himself out. It doesn't matter who he is or what he's done, he is going to be trying to put ethics in on himself, one way or the other.

Even with Hitler and Napoleon, there were attempts at self-restraint. It's interesting in looking at the lives of these people how thoroughly they worked at self-destruction. The self-destruction is their attempt at applying ethics to themselves. They worked at this self-destruction on several dynamics. They can't put ethics in on themselves, they can't restrain themselves from doing these harmful acts, so they punish themselves. They realize they are criminals and cave themselves in.

All beings are basically good and are attempting to survive as best they can. They are attempting to put ethics in on their dynamics.

Ethics and justice were developed and exist to aid an individual in his urge towards survival. They exist to keep the dynamics in communication. The technology of Ethics is the actual technology of survival.

An individual's dynamics will be in communication to the degree that he is applying ethics to his life. If one knows and applies Ethics Technology to his life, he can keep the dynamics in communication and continuously increase his survival.

That is why ethics exists–so that we can survive like we want to survive, by having our dynamics in communication.

Ethics are not to be confused with justice. Justice is used only after a failure of the individual to use ethics on himself. With personal ethics in across the dynamics, justice disappears as a primary concern. That's where you get a world without crime.

A man who steals from his employer has his Third Dynamic out of communication with his First Dynamic. He is headed for a prison sentence, or unemployment at best, which is not what one would call optimum survival on the First and Second Dynamic (not to mention the rest of them). He probably believes he is enhancing his survival by stealing, yet if he knew the technology of Ethics he would realize he is harming himself as well as others and will only end up further down the chute.

The man who lies, the woman who cheats on her husband, the teenager who takes drugs, the politician who is involved in dishonest dealings, all are cutting their own throats. They are harming their own survival by having their dynamics out of communication and not applying ethics to their lives.

It may come as a surprise to you, but a clean heart and clean hands are the only way to achieve happiness and survival. The criminal will never make it unless he reforms; the liar will never be happy or satisfied with himself until he begins dealing in truth.

The optimum solution to any problem presented by life would be that which leads to increased survival on the majority of the dynamics.

Thus we see that a knowledge of ethics is necessary to survival.

The knowledge and application of ethics is the way out of the trap of degradation and pain.

We can, each and every one of us, achieve happiness and optimum survival for ourselves and others by using Ethics Technology.

WHAT HAPPENS IF THE DYNAMICS GO OUT-ETHICS

It is important to remember that these dynamics comprise life. They do not operate singly without interaction with the other dynamics.

Life is a group effort. None survive alone.

If one dynamic goes out-ethics, it goes out of communication with (to a greater or lesser degree) the other dynamics. In order to remain in communication, the dynamics must remain in-ethics.

Let us take the example of a woman who has totally withdrawn from the Third Dynamic. She won't have anything to do with any groups or the people of her town. She has no friends. She stays locked in her house all day thinking (with some misguided idea of independence or individuality) that she is surviving better on her First Dynamic. Actually she is quite unhappy and lonely and lives in fear of other human beings. To ease her misery and boredom, she begins to take sedatives and tranquilizers which she becomes addicted to and then starts drinking alcohol as well.

She is busy "solving" her dilemma with further destructive actions. You can see how she has driven her First, Second and Third Dynamics out of communication. She is actively destroying her survival on her dynamics. These actions are out-ethics in the extreme, and it would not be surprising if she eventually killed herself with the deadly combination of sedatives and alcohol.

Or let us take the man who is committing destructive acts on the job. These acts need not be large, they can be as simple as showing up late for work, not doing as professional a job on each product as he is capable of, damaging equipment or hiding things from his employer. He does not have to be overtly engaged in the total destruction of the company to know that he is committing harmful acts.

Now, this man finds himself sliding more and more out-ethics as time goes along. He feels he must hide more and more and he does not know how to stop this downward spiral. Very likely it never even occurred to him that he could stop it. He is lacking the technology of Ethics. He probably doesn't realize that his actions are driving his dynamics out of communication.

This may affect his other dynamics in various ways. He will probably be a bit miserable and, since he is basically good, he will feel guilt. He goes home at night and his wife says cheerily, "How was your day?" and he cringes a little and feels worse. He starts drinking to numb the misery. He is out of communication with his family. He is out of communication on his job. His performance at work worsens. He begins to neglect himself and his belongings. He no longer gets joy out of life. His happy and satisfying life slips away from him. Because he does not know and apply Ethics Technology to his life and his dynamics, the situation goes quite out of his control. He has unwittingly become the effect of his own out-ethics. Unless he gets his life straightened out by using ethics, he will undoubtedly die a miserable man.

Now I ask you, what kind of life is that? Unfortunately, it is all too common in our current times.

A person cannot go out-ethics on a dynamic without it having disastrous consequences on his other dynamics.

It is really quite tragic, the tragedy being compounded by the fact that it is so unnecessary. If Man only knew the simple technology of Ethics, he could achieve for himself the self-respect, personal satisfaction and success that he only believes himself capable of dreaming of, not attaining.

Man is seeking survival. Survival is measured in pleasure. That means, to most men, happiness, self-respect, the personal satisfaction of a job well done and success. A man may have money, he may have a lot of personal belongings, etc., but he will not be happy unless he actually has his ethics in and knows he came by these things honestly. These rich political and financial criminals are not happy. They may be envied by the common man for their wealth, but they are very unhappy people who more often than not come to grief eventually through drug or alcohol addiction, suicide or some other means of self-destruction.

Let us look at the all-too-common current occurrence of out-ethics on the Second Dynamic. This is generally thought to be perfectly acceptable behavior.

It is easy to see how Second Dynamic out-ethics affects the other dynamics.

Let us say we have a young woman who is somewhat happily married and decides to have an affair with her boss, who happens to be a good friend of her husband. This is quite obviously out-ethics, as well as against the law, although an amazing number of people would find this sort of behavior acceptable or mildly objectionable at most.

This is quite a destructive act, however. She will suffer from guilt; she will feel deceitful and unhappy because she knows she has committed a bad act against her husband. Her relationship with him will certainly suffer and since her boss is experiencing much the same thing in his home, she and her boss will begin to feel bad towards each other as they begin to target each other for their misfortune. Their dynamics end up quite messed up and out of communication. She will feel unhappy on her First Dynamic as she has abandoned her own moral code. Her Second Dynamic will be out of communication and she may even begin to find fault with and dislike her husband. The situation at work is strained as she is now out of communication with her boss and her fellow workers. Her boss has ruined his relationship and friendship with her husband. She is so embroiled in these three dynamics that they go totally out of communication with her Fourth, Fifth and Sixth Dynamics. This is all the result of ethics going out on a single dynamic.

The repercussions spread insidiously to all the dynamics.

Our survival is assured only by our knowledge and application of ethics to our dynamics in order to keep them in communication.

Through ethics we can achieve survival and happiness for ourselves and for planet Earth.

L. Ron Hubbard

In Closing

THE TRUE STORY
OF SCIENTOLOGY

SCIENTOLOGY:
A NEW SLANT ON LIFE

L. RON HUBBARD

"So the true story of Scientology

is a simple story.

And too true to be turned aside."

THE TRUE STORY
OF SCIENTOLOGY

THE TRUE STORY of Scientology is simple, concise and direct. It is quickly told:

1. A philosopher developed a philosophy about life and death.

2. People find it interesting.

3. People find it works.

4. People pass it along to others.

5. It grows.

When we examine this extremely accurate and very brief account, we see that there must be in our civilization some very disturbing elements for anything else to be believed about Scientology.

These disturbing elements are the Merchants of Chaos. They deal in confusion and upset. Their daily bread is made by creating chaos. If chaos were to lessen, so would their incomes.

The politician, the reporter, the medico, the drug manufacturer, the militarist and arms manufacturer, the police and the undertaker, to name the leaders of the list, fatten only upon "the dangerous environment." Even individuals and family members can be Merchants of Chaos.

It is to their interest to make the environment seem as threatening as possible, for only then can they profit. Their incomes, force and power rise in direct ratio to the amount of threat they can inject into the surroundings of the people. With that threat, they can extort revenue, appropriations, heightened circulations and recompense without question. These are the Merchants of Chaos. If they did not generate it and buy and sell it, they would, they suppose, be poor.

For instance, we speak loosely of "good press." Is there any such thing today? Look over a newspaper. Is there anything *good* on the front page? Rather, there is murder and sudden death, disagreement and catastrophe. And even that, bad as it is, is sensationalized to make it seem worse.

This is the cold-blooded manufacture of "a dangerous environment." People do not need this news and if they did, they need the facts, not the upset. But if you hit a person hard enough, he can be made to give up money. That's the basic formula of extortion. That's the way papers are sold. The impact makes them stick.

A paper has to have chaos and confusion. A "news story" has to have "conflict," they say. So there is no good press. There is only *bad* press about everything. To yearn for "good press" is foolhardy in a society where the Merchants of Chaos reign.

Look what has to be done to the true story of Scientology in order to "make it a news story" by modern press standards. Conflict must be injected where there is none. Therefore the press has to dream up upset and conflict.

Let us take the first line. How does one make conflict out of it? "1. A philosopher develops a philosophy about life and death."

The Chaos Merchant *has* to inject one of several possible conflicts here: He is not a philosopher, they have to assert. They are never quite bold enough to say it is not a philosophy. But they can and do go on endlessly, as their purpose compels them, in an effort to invalidate the identity of the person developing it.

In actual fact, the developer of the philosophy was very well grounded in academic subjects and the humanities, probably better grounded in formal philosophy alone than teachers of philosophy in universities. The one-man effort is incredible in terms of study and research hours and is a record never approached in living memory, but this would not be considered newsworthy. To write the simple fact that a philosopher had developed a philosophy is not newspaper-type news and it would not disturb the environment. Hence the elaborate news fictions about (1) above.

Then take the second part of the true story. "People find it interesting." It would be very odd if they didn't, as everyone asks these questions of himself and looks for the answers to his own beingness, and the basic truth of the answers is observable in the conclusions of Scientology.

However, to make this "news," it has to be made disturbing. People are painted as "kidnapped" or "hypnotized" and "dragged as unwilling victims" up to read the books or listen.

The Chaos Merchant leaves (3) very thoroughly alone. It is dangerous ground for him. "People find it works." No hint of workability would ever be attached to Scientology by the press, although there is no doubt in the press mind that it *does* work.

That's why it's dangerous. It calms the environment. So, any time spent trying to convince press Scientology works is time spent upsetting a reporter.

On "4. People pass it along to others," press feels betrayed. Nobody should believe anything they don't read in the papers. How dare word of mouth exist? So to try to stop people from listening, the Chaos Merchant has to use words like "cult." That's a "closed group," whereas Scientology is the most open group on Earth to anyone. And they have to attack organizations and their people to try to keep people out of Scientology.

Now as for "5. It grows," we have the true objection.

As truth goes forward, lies die. The slaughter of lies is an act that takes bread from the mouth of a Chaos Merchant. Unless he can lie with wild abandon about how bad it all is, he thinks he will starve.

The world simply must *not* be a better place according to the Chaos Merchant. If people were less disturbed, less beaten down by their environments, there would be no new appropriations for police and armies and big rockets and there'd be not even pennies for a screaming sensational press.

So long as politicians move upward on scandal, police get more pay for more crime, medicos get fatter on more sickness, there will be Merchants of Chaos. They're paid for it.

And their threat is the simple story of Scientology. For that is the true story. And behind its progress there is a calmer environment in which a man can live and feel better. If you don't believe it, just stop reading newspapers for two weeks and see if you feel better. Suppose you had all such disturbances handled?

The pity of it is, of course, that even the Merchant of Chaos needs us, not to get fatter but just to live himself as a being.

So the true story of Scientology is a simple story.

And too true to be turned aside.

L. Ron Hubbard

Epilogue

My Philosophy · 271

My Philosophy

SCIENTOLOGY:
A NEW SLANT ON LIFE

L. RON HUBBARD

" *I have seen life from the top down*
and the bottom up. I know
how it looks both ways.
And I know there is wisdom
and that there is hope. "

MY PHILOSOPHY

THE SUBJECT of philosophy is very ancient. The word means "the love, study or pursuit of wisdom, or of knowledge of things and their causes, whether theoretical or practical."

All we know of science or of religion comes from philosophy. It lies behind and above all other knowledge we have or use.

For long regarded as a subject reserved for halls of learning and the intellectual, the subject to a remarkable degree has been denied the man in the street.

Surrounded by protective coatings of impenetrable scholarliness, philosophy has been reserved to the privileged few.

The first principle of my own philosophy is that wisdom is meant for anyone who wishes to reach for it. It is the servant of the commoner and king alike and should never be regarded with awe.

Selfish scholars seldom forgive anyone who seeks to break down the walls of mystery and let the people in. Will Durant, the modern American philosopher, was relegated to the scrapheap by his fellow scholars when he wrote a popular book on the subject,

The Story of Philosophy. Thus brickbats come the way of any who seek to bring wisdom to the people over the objections of the "inner circle."

The second principle of my own philosophy is that it must be capable of being applied.

Learning locked in mildewed books is of little use to anyone and therefore of no value unless it can be used.

The third principle is that any philosophic knowledge is only valuable if it is true or if it works.

These three principles are so strange to the field of philosophy that I have given my philosophy a name: *Scientology.* This means only "knowing how to know."

A philosophy can only be a *route* to knowledge. It cannot be knowledge crammed down one's throat. If one has a route, he can then find what is true for him. And that is Scientology.

Know thyself–and the truth shall set you free.

Therefore, in Scientology we are not concerned with individual actions and differences. We are only concerned with how to show Man how he can set himself or herself free.

This, of course, is not very popular with those who depend upon the slavery of others for their living or power. But it happens to be the only way I have found that really improves an individual's life.

Suppression and oppression are the basic causes of depression. If you relieve those, a person can lift his head, become well, become happy with life.

And though it may be unpopular with the slave master, it is very popular with the people. Common Man likes to be happy and well. He likes to be able to understand things. And he knows his route to freedom lies through knowledge.

Therefore, since 1950 I have had Mankind knocking on my door. It has not mattered where I have lived or how remote. Since I first published a book* on the subject, my life has no longer been my own.

I like to help others and count it as my greatest pleasure in life to see a person free himself of the shadows which darken his days.

These shadows look so thick to him and weigh him down so that when he finds they *are* shadows and that he can see through them, walk through them and be again in the sun, he is enormously delighted. And I am afraid I am just as delighted as he is.

I have seen much human misery. As a very young man I wandered through Asia and saw the agony and misery of overpopulated and undereducated lands. I have seen people uncaring and stepping over dying men in the streets. I have seen children less than rags and bones. And amongst this poverty and degradation I found holy places where wisdom was great but where it was carefully hidden and given out only as superstition. Later, in Western universities, I saw Man obsessed with materiality and with all his cunning, I saw him hide what little wisdom he really had in forbidding halls and make it inaccessible to the common and less favored man. I have been through a terrible war and saw its terror and pain uneased by a single word of decency or humanity. I have lived no cloistered life and hold in contempt the wise man who has not *lived* and the scholar who will not share.

Dianetics: The Modern Science of Mental Health, published in May 1950.

There have been many wiser men than I, but few have traveled as much road.

I have seen life from the top down and the bottom up. I know how it looks both ways. And I know there *is* wisdom and that there is hope.

Blinded with injured optic nerves and lame with physical injuries to hip and back at the end of World War II, I faced an almost nonexistent future. My service record states, "This officer has no neurotic or psychotic tendencies of any kind whatsoever," but it also states, "permanently disabled physically." And so there came a further blow–I was abandoned by family and friends as a supposedly hopeless cripple and a probable burden upon them for the rest of my days. I yet worked my way back to fitness and strength in less than two years using only what I knew and could determine about Man and his relationship to the universe. I had no one to help me; what I had to know I had to find out. And it's quite a trick studying when you cannot see. I became used to being told it was all impossible, that there was no way, no hope. Yet I came to see again and walk again and I built an entirely new life. It is a happy life, a busy one and I hope a useful one. My only moments of sadness are those which come when bigoted men tell others all is bad and there is no route anywhere, no hope anywhere, nothing but sadness and sameness and desolation and that every effort to help others is false. I know it is not true.

So my own philosophy is that one should share what wisdom he has, one should help others to help themselves and one should keep going despite heavy weather, for there is always a calm ahead. One should also ignore catcalls from the selfish intellectual who cries, "Don't expose the mystery. Keep it all for ourselves. The people cannot understand."

But as I have never seen wisdom do any good kept to oneself, and as I like to see others happy, and as I find the vast majority of the people can and *do* understand, I will keep on writing and working and teaching so long as I exist.

For I know no man who has any monopoly upon the wisdom of this universe. It belongs to those who can use it to help themselves and others.

If things were a little better known and understood, we would all lead happier lives.

And there is a way to know them and there *is* a way to freedom.

The old must give way to the new, falsehood must become exposed by truth, and truth, though fought, always in the end prevails.

APPENDIX

FURTHER STUDY
BOOKS & LECTURES BY L. RON HUBBARD

The materials of Dianetics and Scientology comprise the largest body of information ever assembled on the mind, spirit and life, rigorously refined and codified by L. Ron Hubbard through five decades of research, investigation and development. The results of that work are contained in hundreds of books and more than 3,000 recorded lectures. A full listing and description of them all can be obtained from any Scientology Church or Publications Organization. (See *Guide to the Materials*.)

The books and lectures below form the foundation upon which the Bridge to Freedom is built. They are listed in the sequence Ron wrote or delivered them. In many instances, Ron gave a series of lectures immediately following the release of a new book to provide further explanation and insight of these milestones. Through monumental restoration efforts, those lectures are now available and are listed herein with their companion book.

While Ron's books contain the summaries of breakthroughs and conclusions as they appeared in the developmental research track, his lectures provide the running day-to-day record of research and explain the thoughts, conclusions, tests and demonstrations that lay along that route. In that regard, they are the complete record of the entire research track, providing not only the most important breakthroughs in Man's history, but the *why* and *how* Ron arrived at them.

Not the least advantage of a chronological study of these books and lectures is the inclusion of words and terms which, when originally used, were defined by LRH with considerable exactitude. Far beyond a mere "definition," entire lectures are devoted to a full description of each new Dianetic or Scientology term—what made the breakthrough possible, its application in auditing as well as its application to life itself. Through a sequential study, you can see how the subject progressed and recognize the highest levels of development. As a result, one leaves behind no misunderstoods, obtains a full conceptual understanding of Dianetics and Scientology and grasps the subjects at a level not otherwise possible.

This is the path to knowing how to know, unlocking the gates to your future eternity. Follow it.

DIANETICS: THE ORIGINAL THESIS • Ron's *first* description of Dianetics. Originally circulated in manuscript form, it was soon copied and passed from hand to hand. Ensuing word of mouth created such demand for more information, Ron concluded the only way to answer the inquiries was with a book. That book was Dianetics: The Modern Science of Mental Health, now the all-time self-help bestseller. Find out what started it all. For here is the bedrock foundation of Dianetic discoveries: the *Original Axioms*, the *Dynamic Principle of Existence*, the *Anatomy of the Analytical* and *Reactive Mind*, the *Dynamics*, the *Tone Scale*, the *Auditor's Code* and the first description of a *Clear*. Even more than that, here are the primary laws describing *how* and *why* auditing works. It's only here in Dianetics: The Original Thesis.

DIANETICS: THE EVOLUTION OF A SCIENCE • This is the story of *how* Ron discovered the reactive mind and developed the procedures to get rid of it. Originally written for a national magazine–published to coincide with the release of Dianetics: The Modern Science of Mental Health–it started a wildfire movement virtually overnight upon that book's publication. Here then are both the fundamentals of Dianetics as well as the only account of Ron's two-decade journey of discovery and how he applied a scientific methodology to the problems of the human mind. He wrote it so you would know. Hence, this book is a must for every Dianeticist and Scientologist.

DIANETICS: THE MODERN SCIENCE OF MENTAL HEALTH • The bolt from the blue that began a worldwide movement. For while Ron had previously announced his discovery of the reactive mind, it had only fueled the fire of those wanting more information. More to the point–it was humanly impossible for one man to clear an entire planet. Encompassing all his previous discoveries and case histories of those breakthroughs in application, Ron provided the complete handbook of Dianetics procedure to train auditors to use it everywhere. A bestseller for more than half a century and with tens of millions of copies in print, Dianetics: The Modern Science of Mental Health has been translated in more than fifty languages, and used in more than 100 countries of Earth–indisputably, the most widely read and influential book about the human mind ever written. And that is why it will forever be known as *Book One*.

DIANETICS LECTURES AND DEMONSTRATIONS • Immediately following the publication of *Dianetics*, LRH began lecturing to packed auditoriums across America. Although addressing thousands at a time, demand continued to grow. To meet that demand, his presentation in Oakland, California, was recorded. In these four lectures, Ron related the events that sparked his investigation and his personal journey to his groundbreaking discoveries. He followed it all with a personal demonstration of Dianetics auditing–the only such demonstration of Book One available. *4 lectures.*

DIANETICS PROFESSIONAL COURSE LECTURES–*A SPECIAL COURSE FOR BOOK ONE AUDITORS* • Following six months of coast-to-coast travel, lecturing to the first Dianeticists, Ron assembled auditors in Los Angeles for a new Professional Course. The subject was his next sweeping discovery on life–the *ARC Triangle,* describing the interrelationship of *Affinity, Reality* and *Communication.* Through a series of fifteen lectures, LRH announced many firsts, including the *Spectrum of Logic,* containing an infinity of gradients from right to wrong; *ARC and the Dynamics;* the *Tone Scales of ARC;* the *Auditor's Code* and how it relates to ARC; and the *Accessibility Chart* that classifies a case and how to process it. Here, then, is both the final statement on Book One Auditing Procedures and the discovery upon which all further research would advance. The data in these lectures was thought to be lost for over fifty years and only available in student notes published in Notes on the Lectures. The original recordings have now been discovered making them broadly available for the first time. Life in its highest state, *Understanding,* is composed of Affinity, Reality and Communication. And, as LRH said, the best description of the ARC Triangle to be found anywhere is in these lectures. *15 lectures.*

SCIENCE OF SURVIVAL–*PREDICTION OF HUMAN BEHAVIOR* • The most useful book you will ever own. Built around the *Hubbard Chart of Human Evaluation,* Science of Survival provides the first accurate prediction of human behavior. Included on the chart are all the manifestations of an individual's survival potential graduated from highest to lowest, making this the complete book on the Tone Scale. Knowing only one or two characteristics of a person and using this chart, you can plot his or her position on the Tone Scale and thereby know the rest, obtaining an accurate index of their *entire* personality, conduct and character. Before this book the world was convinced that cases could not improve but only deteriorate. Science of Survival presents the idea of different states of case and the brand-new idea that one can progress upward on the Tone Scale. And therein lies the basis of today's Grade Chart.

THE SCIENCE OF SURVIVAL LECTURES • Underlying the development of the Tone Scale and Chart of Human Evaluation was a monumental breakthrough: The *Theta-MEST Theory,* containing the explanation of the interaction between Life–*theta*–with the physical universe of Matter, Energy, Space and Time–*MEST.* In these lectures, delivered to students immediately following publication of the book, Ron gave the most expansive description of all that lies behind the Chart of Human Evaluation and its application in life itself. Moreover, here also is the explanation of how the ratio of *theta* and *en(turbulated)-theta* determines one's position on the Tone Scale and the means to ascend to higher states. *4 lectures.*

SELF ANALYSIS • The barriers of life are really just shadows. Learn to know yourself–not just a shadow of yourself. Containing the most complete description of consciousness, Self Analysis takes you through your past, through your potentials, your life. First, with a series of self-examinations and using a special version of the Hubbard Chart of Human Evaluation, you plot yourself on the Tone Scale. Then, applying a series of light yet powerful processes, you embark on the great adventure of self-discovery. This book further contains embracive principles that reach *any* case, from the lowest to the highest–including auditing techniques so effective they are referred to by Ron again and again through all following years of research into the highest states. In sum, this book not only moves one up the Tone Scale but can pull a person out of almost anything.

ADVANCED PROCEDURE AND AXIOMS • With new breakthroughs on the nature and anatomy of engrams–"Engrams are effective only when the individual himself determines that they will be effective"–came the discovery of the being's use of a *Service Facsimile:* a mechanism employed to explain away failures in life, but which then locks a person into detrimental patterns of behavior and further failure. In consequence came a new type of processing addressing *Thought, Emotion* and *Effort* detailed in the "Fifteen Acts" of Advanced Procedure and oriented to the rehabilitation of the preclear's *Self-determinism*. Hence, this book also contains the all-encompassing, no-excuses-allowed explanation of *Full Responsibility,* the key to unlocking it all. Moreover, here is the codification of *Definitions, Logics,* and *Axioms,* providing both the summation of the entire subject and direction for all future research. *See Handbook for Preclears, written as a companion self-processing manual to Advanced Procedure and Axioms.*

> **THOUGHT, EMOTION AND EFFORT** • With the codification of the Axioms came the means to address key points on a case that could unravel all aberration. *Basic Postulates, Prime Thought, Cause and Effect* and their effect on everything from *memory* and *responsibility* to an individual's own role in empowering *engrams*–these matters are only addressed in this series. Here, too, is the most complete description of the *Service Facsimile* found anywhere–and why its resolution removes an individual's self-imposed disabilities. *21 lectures.*

HANDBOOK FOR PRECLEARS • The "Fifteen Acts" of Advanced Procedure and Axioms are paralleled by the fifteen Self-processing Acts given in Handbook for Preclears. Moreover, this book contains several essays giving the most expansive description of the *Ideal State of Man*. Discover why behavior patterns become so solidly fixed; why habits seemingly can't be broken; how decisions long ago have more power over a person than his decisions today; and why a person keeps past negative experiences in the present. It's all clearly laid out on the Chart of Attitudes–a milestone breakthrough that complements the Chart of Human Evaluation–plotting the ideal state of being and one's *attitudes* and *reactions* to life. *In self-processing, Handbook for Preclears is used in conjunction with Self Analysis.*

THE LIFE CONTINUUM • Besieged with requests for lectures on his latest breakthroughs, Ron replied with everything they wanted and more at the Second Annual Conference of Dianetic Auditors. Describing the technology that lies behind the self-processing steps of the *Handbook*–here is the *how* and *why* of it all: the discovery of *Life Continuum*–the mechanism by which an individual is compelled to carry on the life of another deceased or departed individual, generating in his own body the infirmities and mannerisms of the departed. Combined with auditor instruction on use of the Chart of Attitudes in determining how to enter every case at the proper gradient, here, too, are directions for dissemination of the Handbook and hence, the means to begin wide-scale clearing. *10 lectures.*

SCIENTOLOGY: MILESTONE ONE • Ron began the first lecture in this series with six words that would change the world forever: "This is a course in *Scientology*." From there, Ron not only described the vast scope of this, a then brand-new subject, he also detailed his discoveries on past lives. He proceeded from there to the description of the first E-Meter and its initial use in uncovering the *theta line* (the entire track of a thetan's existence), as entirely distinct from the *genetic body line* (the time track of bodies and their physical evolution), shattering the "one-life" lie and revealing the *whole track* of spiritual existence. Here, then, is the very genesis of Scientology. *22 lectures.*

THE ROUTE TO INFINITY: TECHNIQUE 80 LECTURES • As Ron explained, "Technique 80 is the *To Be or Not To Be* Technique." With that, he unveiled the crucial foundation on which ability and sanity rest: *the being's capacity to make a decision.* Here, then, is the anatomy of "maybe," the *Wavelengths of ARC*, the *Tone Scale of Decisions,* and the means to rehabilitate a being's ability *To Be*…almost *anything. 7 lectures. (Knowledge of Technique 80 is required for Technique 88 as described in Scientology: A History of Man–below.)*

SCIENTOLOGY: A HISTORY OF MAN • "A cold-blooded and factual account of your last 76 trillion years." So begins A History of Man, announcing the revolutionary *Technique 88*—revealing for the first time the truth about whole track experience and the exclusive address, in auditing, to the thetan. Here is history unraveled with the first E-Meter, delineating and describing the principal incidents on the whole track to be found in any human being: *Electronic implants, entities, the genetic track, between-lives incidents, how bodies evolved and why you got trapped in them*—they're all detailed here.

TECHNIQUE 88: INCIDENTS ON THE TRACK BEFORE EARTH • "Technique 88 is the most hyperbolical, effervescent, dramatic, unexaggeratable, high-flown, superlative, grandiose, colossal and magnificent technique which the mind of Man could conceivably embrace. It is as big as the whole track and all the incidents on it. It's what you apply it to; it's what's been going on. It contains the riddles and secrets, the mysteries of all time. You could bannerline this technique like they do a sideshow, but nothing you could say, no adjective you could use, would adequately describe even a small segment of it. It not only batters the imagination, it makes you ashamed to imagine anything," is Ron's introduction to you in this never-before-available lecture series, expanding on all else contained in History of Man. What awaits you is the whole track itself. *15 lectures.*

SCIENTOLOGY 8-80 • The *first* explanation of the electronics of human thought and the energy phenomena in any being. Discover how even physical universe laws of motion are mirrored in a being, not to mention the electronics of aberration. Here is the link between theta and MEST revealing what energy *is,* and how you *create* it. It was this breakthrough that revealed the subject of a thetan's *flows* and which, in turn, is applied in *every* auditing process today. In the book's title, "8-8" stands for *Infinity-Infinity,* and "0" represents the static, *theta.* Included are the *Wavelengths of Emotion, Aesthetics, Beauty and Ugliness, Inflow and Outflow* and the *Sub-zero Tone Scale*—applicable only to the thetan.

SOURCE OF LIFE ENERGY • Beginning with the announcement of his new book – Scientology 8-80 – Ron not only unveiled his breakthroughs of theta as the Source of Life Energy, but detailed the *Methods of Research* he used to make that and every other discovery of Dianetics and Scientology: the *Qs* and *Logics*—methods of *thinking* applicable to any universe or thinking process. Here, then, is both *how to think* and *how to evaluate all data and knowledge,* and thus, the linchpin to a full understanding of both Scientology and life itself. *14 lectures.*

THE COMMAND OF THETA • While in preparation of his newest book and the Doctorate Course he was about to deliver, Ron called together auditors for a new Professional Course. As he said, "For the first time with this class we are stepping, really, beyond the scope of the word *Survival*." From that vantage point, the Command of Theta gives the technology that bridges the knowledge from 8-80 to 8-8008, and provides the first full explanation of the subject of *Cause* and a permanent shift of orientation in life from MEST to *Theta*. *10 lectures.*

SCIENTOLOGY **8-8008** • The complete description of the behavior and potentials of a *thetan*, and textbook for the Philadelphia Doctorate Course and The Factors: Admiration and the Renaissance of Beingness lectures. As Ron said, the book's title serves to fix in the mind of the individual a route by which he can rehabilitate himself, his abilities, his ethics and his goals—the attainment of *infinity* (8) by the reduction of the apparent *infinity* (8) of the MEST universe to *zero* (0) and the increase of the apparent *zero* (0) of one's own universe to *infinity* (8). Condensed herein are more than 80,000 hours of investigation, with a summarization and amplification of every breakthrough to date—and the full significance of those discoveries form the new vantage point of *Operating Thetan*.

THE PHILADELPHIA DOCTORATE COURSE LECTURES • This renowned series stands as the largest single body of work on the anatomy, behavior and potentials of the spirit of Man ever assembled, providing the very fundamentals which underlie the route to Operating Thetan. Here it is in complete detail—the thetan's relationship to the *creation, maintenance* and *destruction of universes*. In just those terms, here is the *anatomy* of matter, energy, space and time, and *postulating* universes into existence. Here, too, is the thetan's fall from whole track abilities and the *universal laws* by which they are restored. In short, here is Ron's codification of the upper echelon of theta beingness and behavior. Lecture after lecture fully expands every concept of the course text, Scientology 8-8008, providing the total scope of *you* in native state. *76 lectures and accompanying reproductions of the original 54 LRH hand-drawn lecture charts.*

THE FACTORS: ADMIRATION AND THE RENAISSANCE OF BEINGNESS • With the *potentials* of a thetan fully established came a look outward resulting in Ron's monumental discovery of a *universal solvent* and the basic laws of the theta *universe*—laws quite literally senior to anything: *The Factors: Summation of the Considerations of the Human Spirit and Material Universe*. So dramatic were these breakthroughs, Ron expanded the book Scientology 8-8008, both clarifying previous discoveries and adding chapter after chapter which, studied with these lectures, provide a postgraduate level to the Doctorate Course. Here then are lectures containing the knowledge of *universal truth* unlocking the riddle of creation itself. *18 lectures.*

THE CREATION OF HUMAN ABILITY—*A HANDBOOK FOR SCIENTOLOGISTS* • On the heels of his discoveries of Operating Thetan came a year of intensive research, exploring the realm of a *thetan exterior.* Through auditing and instruction, including 450 lectures in this same twelve-month span, Ron codified the entire subject of Scientology. And it's all contained in this handbook, from a *Summary of Scientology* to its basic *Axioms* and *Codes*. Moreover, here is *Intensive Procedure,* containing the famed Exteriorization Processes of *Route 1* and *Route 2*–processes drawn right from the Axioms. Each one is described in detail–*how* the process is used, *why* it works, the axiomatic technology that underlies its use, and the complete explanation of how a being can break the *false agreements* and *self-created barriers* that enslave him to the physical universe. In short, this book contains the ultimate summary of thetan exterior OT ability and its permanent accomplishment.

> **PHOENIX LECTURES: FREEING THE HUMAN SPIRIT** • Here is the panoramic view of Scientology complete. Having codified the subject of Scientology in Creation of Human Ability, Ron then delivered a series of half-hour lectures to specifically accompany a full study of the book. From the *essentials* that underlie the technology–*The Axioms, Conditions of Existence* and *Considerations and Mechanics,* to the processes of *Intensive Procedure,* including twelve lectures describing one-by-one the thetan exterior processes of *Route 1*–it's all covered in full, providing a conceptual understanding of the *science of knowledge* and *native state OT ability.* Here then are the bedrock principles upon which everything in Scientology rests, including the embracive statement of the religion and its heritage–*Scientology, Its General Background.* Hence, this is the watershed lecture series on Scientology itself, and the axiomatic foundation for all future research. *42 lectures.*

DIANETICS 55!–*THE COMPLETE MANUAL OF HUMAN COMMUNICATION* • With all breakthroughs to date, a single factor had been isolated as crucial to success in every type of auditing. As LRH said, "Communication is so thoroughly important today in Dianetics and Scientology (as it always has been on the whole track) that it could be said if you were to get a preclear into communication, you would get him well." And this book delineates the *exact,* but previously unknown, anatomy and formulas for *perfect* communication. The magic of the communication cycle is *the* fundamental of auditing and the primary reason auditing works. The breakthroughs here opened new vistas of application–discoveries of such magnitude, LRH called Dianetics 55! the *Second Book* of Dianetics.

> **THE UNIFICATION CONGRESS: COMMUNICATION! FREEDOM & ABILITY** • The historic Congress announcing the reunification of the subjects of Dianetics and Scientology with the release of *Dianetics 55!* Until now, each had operated in their own sphere: Dianetics addressed Man *as Man*–the first four dynamics, while Scientology addressed *life itself*–the Fifth to Eighth Dynamics. The formula which would serve as the foundation for all future development was contained in a single word: *Communication.* It was a paramount breakthrough Ron would later call, "the great discovery of Dianetics and Scientology." Here, then, are the lectures, as it happened. *16 lectures and accompanying reproductions of the original LRH hand-drawn lecture charts.*

SCIENTOLOGY: THE FUNDAMENTALS OF THOUGHT–*THE BASIC BOOK OF THE THEORY AND PRACTICE OF SCIENTOLOGY FOR BEGINNERS* • Designated by Ron as the *Book One of Scientology.* After having fully unified and codified the subjects of Dianetics and Scientology came the refinement of their *fundamentals.* Originally published as a résumé of Scientology for use in translations into non-English tongues, this book is of inestimable value to both the beginner and advanced student of the mind, spirit and life. Equipped with this book alone, one can begin a practice and perform seeming miracle changes in the states of well-being, ability and intelligence of people. Contained within are the *Conditions of Existence, Eight Dynamics, ARC Triangle, Parts of Man,* the full analysis of *Life as a Game,* and more, including exact processes for individual application of these principles in processing. Here, then, in one book, is the starting point for bringing Scientology to people everywhere.

HUBBARD PROFESSIONAL COURSE LECTURES • While Fundamentals of Thought stands as an introduction to the subject for beginners, it also contains a distillation of fundamentals for every Scientologist. Here are the in-depth descriptions of those fundamentals, each lecture one-half hour in length and providing, one-by-one, a complete mastery of a single Scientology breakthrough–*Axioms 1-10; The Anatomy of Control; Handling of Problems; Start, Change and Stop; Confusion and Stable Data; Exteriorization; Valences* and more–the *why* behind them, *how* they came to be and their mechanics. And it's all brought together with the *Code of a Scientologist,* point by point, and its use in actually creating a new civilization. In short, here are the LRH lectures that make a *Professional Scientologist*–one who can apply the subject to every aspect of life. *21 lectures.*

Additional Books
Containing Scientology Essentials

Work

The Problems of Work–*Scientology Applied to the Workaday World* • Having codified the entire subject of Scientology, Ron immediately set out to provide the *beginning* manual for its application by anyone. As he described it: life is composed of seven-tenths work, one-tenth familial, one-tenth political and one-tenth relaxation. Here, then, is Scientology applied to that seven-tenths of existence including the answers to *Exhaustion* and the *Secret of Efficiency*. Here, too, is the analysis of life itself–a game composed of exact rules. Know them and you succeed. Problems of Work contains technology no one can live without, and that can immediately be applied by both the Scientologist and those new to the subject.

Life Principles

Scientology: A New Slant on Life • *(This current volume.)* Scientology essentials for every aspect of life. Basic answers that put you in charge of your existence, truths to consult again and again: *Is It Possible to Be Happy?, Two Rules for Happy Living, Personal Integrity, The Anti-Social Personality* and many more. In every part of this book you will find Scientology truths that describe conditions in your life and furnish *exact* ways to improve them. Scientology: A New Slant on Life contains essential knowledge for every Scientologist and a perfect introduction for anyone new to the subject.

Axioms, Codes and Scales

Scientology 0-8: The Book of Basics • The companion to *all* Ron's books, lectures and materials. This is *the* Book of Basics, containing indispensable data you will refer to constantly: the *Axioms of Dianetics and Scientology; The Factors;* a full compilation of all *Scales*–more than 100 in all; listings of the *Perceptics* and *Awareness Levels;* all *Codes* and *Creeds* and much more. The senior laws of existence are condensed into this single volume, distilled from more than 15,000 pages of writings, 3,000 lectures and scores of books.

SCIENTOLOGY ETHICS:
TECHNOLOGY OF OPTIMUM SURVIVAL

INTRODUCTION TO SCIENTOLOGY ETHICS • A new hope for Man arises with the first workable technology of ethics–technology to help an individual pull himself out of the downward skid of life and to a higher plateau of survival. This is the comprehensive handbook providing the crucial fundamentals: *Basics of Ethics & Justice; Honesty; Conditions of Existence; Condition Formulas* from Confusion to Power; the *Basics of Suppression* and its handling; as well as *Justice Procedures* and their use in Scientology Churches. Here, then, is the technology to overcome any barriers in life and in one's personal journey up the Bridge to Total Freedom.

PURIFICATION

CLEAR BODY, CLEAR MIND–*THE EFFECTIVE PURIFICATION PROGRAM* • We live in a biochemical world, and this book is the solution. While investigating the harmful effects that earlier drug use had on preclears' cases, Ron made the major discovery that many street drugs, particularly LSD, remained in a person's body long after ingested. Residues of the drug, he noted, could have serious and lasting effects, including triggering further "trips." Additional research revealed that a wide range of substances–medical drugs, alcohol, pollutants, household chemicals and even food preservatives–could also lodge in the body's tissues. Through research on thousands of cases, he developed the *Purification Program* to eliminate their destructive effects. Clear Body, Clear Mind details every aspect of the all-natural regimen that can free one from the harmful effects of drugs and other toxins, opening the way for spiritual progress.

REFERENCE HANDBOOKS

WHAT IS SCIENTOLOGY?

The complete and essential encyclopedic reference on the subject and practice of Scientology. Organized for use, this book contains the pertinent data on every aspect of the subject:

• The life of L. Ron Hubbard and his path of discovery

• The Spiritual Heritage of the religion

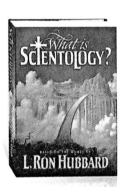

• A full description of Dianetics and Scientology

• Auditing–what it is and how it works

• Courses–what they contain and how they are structured

• The Grade Chart of Services and how one ascends to higher states

• The Scientology Ethics and Justice System

• The Organizational Structure of the Church

• A complete description of the many Social Betterment programs supported by the Church, including: Drug Rehabilitation, Criminal Reform, Literacy and Education and the instilling of real values for morality

Over 1,000 pages in length, with more than 500 photographs and illustrations, this text further includes Creeds, Codes, a full listing of all books and materials as well as a Catechism with answers to virtually any question regarding the subject.

You Ask and This Book Answers.

THE SCIENTOLOGY HANDBOOK

Scientology fundamentals for daily use in every part of life. Encompassing 19 separate bodies of technology, here is the most comprehensive manual on the basics of life ever published. Each chapter contains key principles and technology for your continual use:

• Study Technology

• The Dynamics of Existence

• The Components of Understanding– Affinity, Reality and Communication

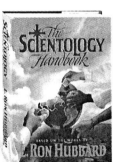

• The Tone Scale

• Communication and its Formulas

• Assists for Illnesses and Injuries

• How to Resolve Conflicts

• Integrity and Honesty

• Ethics and Condition Formulas

• Answers to Suppression and a Dangerous Environment

• Marriage

• Children

• Tools for the Workplace

More than 700 photographs and illustrations make it easy for you to learn the procedures and apply them at once. This book is truly the indispensable handbook for every Scientologist.

The Technology to Build a Better World.

ABOUT L. RON HUBBARD

To really know life," L. Ron Hubbard wrote, "you've got to be part of life. You must get down and look, you must get into the nooks and crannies of existence. You have to rub elbows with all kinds and types of men before you can finally establish what he is."

Through his long and extraordinary journey to the founding of Dianetics and Scientology, Ron did just that. From his adventurous youth in a rough and tumble American West to his far-flung trek across a still mysterious Asia; from his two-decade search for the very essence of life to the triumph of Dianetics and Scientology–such are the stories recounted in the L. Ron Hubbard Biographical Publications.

Presenting the photographic overview of Ron's greater journey is *L. Ron Hubbard: Images of a Lifetime*. Drawn from his own archival collection, this is Ron's life as he himself saw it.

While for the many aspects of that rich and varied life, stands the Ron Series. Each issue focuses on a specific LRH profession: *Auditor, Humanitarian, Philosopher, Artist, Poet, Music Maker, Photographer* and many more including his published articles on *Freedom* and his personal *Letters & Journals*. Here is the life of a man who lived at least twenty lives in the space of one.

FOR FURTHER INFORMATION VISIT
www.lronhubbard.org

GUIDE TO THE MATERIALS

YOU'RE ON AN ADVENTURE!
HERE'S THE MAP.

- All books
- All lectures
- All reference books

All of it
laid out in
chronological
sequence with
descriptions of
what each
contains.

Your journey to a full understanding of Dianetics and Scientology is the greatest adventure of all. But you need a map that shows you where you are and where you are going.

That map is the Materials Guide Chart. It shows all Ron's books and lectures with a full description of their content and subject matter so you can find exactly what *you* are looking for and precisely what *you* need.

Since each book and lecture is laid out in chronological sequence, you can see *how* the subjects of Dianetics and Scientology were developed. And what that means is by simply studying this chart you are in for cognition after cognition!

New editions of all books include extensive glossaries, containing definitions for every technical term. And as a result of a monumental restoration program, the entire library of Ron's lectures are being made available on compact disc, with complete transcripts, glossaries, lecture graphs, diagrams and issues he refers to in the lectures. As a result, you get *all* the data, and can learn with ease, gaining a full *conceptual* understanding.

And what that adds up to is a new Golden Age of Knowledge every Dianeticist and Scientologist has dreamed of.

To obtain your FREE Materials Guide Chart and Catalog, or to order L. Ron Hubbard's books and lectures, contact:

WESTERN HEMISPHERE:

Bridge Publications, Inc.

4751 Fountain Avenue
Los Angeles, CA 90029 USA
www.bridgepub.com
Phone: 1-800-722-1733
Fax: 1-323-953-3328

EASTERN HEMISPHERE:

New Era Publications International ApS

Store Kongensgade 53
1264 Copenhagen K, Denmark
www.newerapublications.com
Phone: (45) 33 73 66 66
Fax: (45) 33 73 66 33

Books and lectures are also available direct from Churches of Scientology.
*See **Addresses**.*

ADDRESSES

Scientology is the fastest-growing religion in the world today. Churches and Missions exist in cities throughout the world, and new ones are continually forming.

To obtain more information or to locate the Church nearest you, visit the Scientology website:

www.scientology.org
e-mail: info@scientology.org

or

Phone: 1-800-334-LIFE
(for US and Canada)

You can also write to any one of the Continental Organizations, listed on the following page, who can direct you to one of the thousands of Churches and Missions world over.

L. Ron Hubbard's books and lectures may be obtained from any of these addresses or direct from the publishers on the previous page.

CONTINENTAL CHURCH ORGANIZATIONS:

UNITED STATES

CHURCH OF SCIENTOLOGY
CONTINENTAL LIAISON OFFICE
WESTERN UNITED STATES
1308 L. Ron Hubbard Way
Los Angeles, California 90027 USA
info@wus.scientology.org

CHURCH OF SCIENTOLOGY
CONTINENTAL LIAISON OFFICE
EASTERN UNITED STATES
349 W. 48th Street
New York, New York 10036 USA
info@eus.scientology.org

CANADA

CHURCH OF SCIENTOLOGY
CONTINENTAL LIAISON OFFICE
CANADA
696 Yonge Street, 2nd Floor
Toronto, Ontario
Canada M4Y 2A7
info@scientology.ca

LATIN AMERICA

CHURCH OF SCIENTOLOGY
CONTINENTAL LIAISON OFFICE
LATIN AMERICA
Federacion Mexicana de Dianetica
Calle Puebla #31
Colonia Roma, Mexico D.F.
C.P. 06700, Mexico
info@scientology.org.mx

UNITED KINGDOM

CHURCH OF SCIENTOLOGY
CONTINENTAL LIAISON OFFICE
UNITED KINGDOM
Saint Hill Manor
East Grinstead, West Sussex
England, RH19 4JY
info@scientology.org.uk

AFRICA

CHURCH OF SCIENTOLOGY
CONTINENTAL LIAISON OFFICE AFRICA
5 Cynthia Street
Kensington
Johannesburg 2094, South Africa
info@scientology.org.za

AUSTRALIA, NEW ZEALAND & OCEANIA
CHURCH OF SCIENTOLOGY
CONTINENTAL LIAISON OFFICE ANZO
16 Dorahy Street
Dundas, New South Wales 2117
Australia
info@scientology.org.au

Church of Scientology Liaison Office of Taiwan
1st, No. 231, Cisian 2nd Road
Kaoshiung City
Taiwan, ROC
info@scientology.org.tw

EUROPE
CHURCH OF SCIENTOLOGY
CONTINENTAL LIAISON OFFICE EUROPE
Store Kongensgade 55
1264 Copenhagen K, Denmark
info@scientology.org.dk

Church of Scientology Liaison Office of Commonwealth of Independent States
Management Center of Dianetics
and Scientology Dissemination
Pervomajskaya Street, House 1A
Korpus Grazhdanskoy Oboroni
Losino-Petrovsky Town
141150 Moscow, Russia
info@scientology.ru

Church of Scientology Liaison Office of Central Europe
1082 Leonardo da Vinci u. 8-14
Budapest, Hungary
info@scientology.hu

Church of Scientology Liaison Office of Iberia
C/Miguel Menendez Boneta, 18
28460 - Los Molinos
Madrid, Spain
info@spain.scientology.org

Church of Scientology Liaison Office of Italy
Via Cadorna, 61
20090 Vimodrone
Milan, Italy
info@scientology.it

Become a Member
of the International
Association of Scientologists

The International Association of Scientologists is the membership organization of all Scientologists united in the most vital crusade on Earth.

A free Six-Month Introductory Membership is extended to anyone who has not held a membership with the Association before.

As a member, you are eligible for discounts on Scientology materials offered only to IAS Members. You also receive the Association magazine, *IMPACT*, issued six times a year, full of Scientology news from around the world.

The purpose of the IAS is:

"To unite, advance, support and protect Scientology and Scientologists in all parts of the world so as to achieve the Aims of Scientology as originated by L. Ron Hubbard."

Join the strongest force for positive change on the planet today, opening the lives of millions to the greater truth embodied in Scientology.

Join the International
Association of Scientologists.

To apply for membership,
write to the International
Association of Scientologists
c/o Saint Hill Manor, East Grinstead
West Sussex, England, RH19 4JY

www.iasmembership.org

Editor's Glossary
of Words, Terms and Phrases

Words often have several meanings. The definitions used here only give the meaning that the word has as it is used in this book. Dianetics and Scientology terms appear in bold type. Beside each definition you will find the page on which it first appears, so you can refer back to the text if you wish.

This glossary is not meant to take the place of standard language or Dianetics and Scientology dictionaries, which should be referred to for any words, terms or phrases that do not appear below.

—The Editors

abandon: 1. give up or withdraw from something. Page 104.
2. a careless or uncontrolled way of behaving, without thinking or caring about what one is doing. Page 149.

aberrated: affected by *aberration*. Aberrated conduct would be wrong conduct, or conduct not supported by reason. Aberration is a departure from rational thought or behavior; not sane. Page 62.

aberration(s): departure from rational thought or behavior; not sane. From the Latin, *aberrare,* to wander from; Latin, *ab,* away, *errare,* to wander. It means basically to err, to make mistakes, or more specifically to have fixed ideas which are not true. The entire cause of aberration is contained in the discovery of the previously unknown *reactive mind.* Its entire anatomy, and the eradication of its harmful effects (that cause aberration), are contained in the book *Dianetics: The Modern Science of Mental Health.* Page 73.

A-bomb: short for *atomic bomb,* an extremely destructive type of bomb, the power of which results from the immense quantity of energy suddenly released with the splitting of the nuclei (centers) of atoms into several fragments. Page 74.

abrasion(s): a damaged area of the skin where it has been rubbed against something hard and rough. Page 26.

absolute: something that is perfect or complete and free from conditions, limitations or gradations; operating or existing in full under all circumstances without variation or exception. Page 37.

absolutes: those things, conditions, etc., which are perfect and complete in quality or nature. Page 240.

accidents: things that happen by chance or without apparent cause. Page 113.

adoration: the exhibition of high regard and deep love. Also the act of worship. Page 47.

adrift: lacking aim, direction or stability. Page 39.

affinity: love, liking or any other emotional attitude. Affinity is conceived, in Scientology, to be something of many facets. Affinity is a variable quality. Affinity is here used as a word with the context "degree of liking." It is one of the three parts of A-R-C (affinity, reality and communication). Page 91.

affinity, reality and communication: affinity, reality and communication (A-R-C) *are* understanding. They form a triangle that is the common denominator to all of life's activities. These three are interdependent one upon the other. One has to have some degree of liking to be able to talk (communicate). Communication is possible only with an agreement of some kind. And agreement is possible only where there is affinity of some kind or type. When one increases communication, one raises affinity and reality. Page 91.

agent: 1. a means by which something is done or caused. Page 26.
2. a person who acts in an official capacity for a government or private agency, as a guard, detective or spy. Page 196.

Age of Miracles: a particular period of history marked by miracles. An allusion to the early era of the Christian Church, in which many miracles are said to have been performed, both by Jesus and his followers, as recounted in the Bible. Page 27.

ally(ies): 1. associate or connect by some mutual relationship; befriend. Page 59.
2. an individual who helps or cooperates with another; a supporter or associate. Page 59.

amassing: gathering for oneself; accumulating (a large amount of something) over a period of time. Page 242.

American Medical Association: a physicians' organization in the United States, founded in 1847. Page 157.

anatomy: structure or arrangement of the parts of something. Page 105.

anew: once more; again. Page 62.

antibiotics: substances that are able to kill or inactivate bacteria in the body. Antibiotics are derived from microorganisms (very small living organisms) or are synthetically produced. Page 26.

antipathetic: feeling or expressing anger, hostility, strong opposition or disgust, especially toward a particular person or thing. Page 103.

anti-social: hostile to or disruptive of the established social order; of behavior that is harmful to the welfare of people generally; averse to society or companionship; unwilling or unable to associate in a normal or friendly way with other people; antagonistic, hostile or unfriendly toward others; menacing; threatening. Page 164.

apathy: a complete lack of emotion for or interest in things generally; an inability to respond emotionally. An individual in apathy has no energy. Page 40.

appropriations: sums of money that have been set aside from a budget, especially a government budget, for a particular purpose. Page 260.

approximate: come near to; approach closely. Page 94.

apt: inclined; disposed to; given to; likely. Page 237.

arbitrary: based on judgment or useful selection rather than on the fixed nature of something. Page 84.

A-R-C: affinity, reality and communication (A-R-C) *are* understanding. They form a triangle that is the common denominator to all of life's activities. These three are interdependent one upon the other. One has to have some degree of liking to be able to talk (communicate). Communication is possible only with an agreement of some kind. And agreement is possible only where there is affinity of some kind or type. When one increases communication, one raises affinity and reality. Page 91.

arduous: severe or demanding. Page 27.

arsonists: persons who purposely and maliciously set fire to buildings or other property. Page 174.

arthritis: acute or chronic inflammation of the joints, causing pain, swelling and stiffness. Page 73.

Asia: the largest continent on Earth, situated in the Eastern Hemisphere, bounded by the Arctic, Pacific and Indian Oceans, and separated from Europe by the Ural Mountains. It includes, in addition to the nations on the land mass, Japan, the Philippines, Taiwan, Malaysia and Indonesia. Page 27.

aspirant: a person who seeks or hopes to attain something, as one who eagerly desires a career, advancement, etc. Page 116.

assertion: a confident and forceful statement of fact or belief. Page 99.

assimilate(d): to absorb as one's own; take into the mind and consider and thoroughly understand. Page 37.

assuredly: for certain, without a doubt. Page 122.

at large: as a whole; in general. Page 228.

at length: after a time; finally. Page 228.

atom bomb: an extremely destructive type of bomb, the power of which results from the splitting of the nuclei (centers) of atoms into fragments, accompanied by a tremendous release of energy. Page 12.

at once: 1. at the same time; simultaneously. Page 86.
2. immediately; straightaway without any delay. Page 93.

attain: to succeed in reaching; to reach a condition or purpose. Page 25.

attend: take care of; treat. Page 242.

attendant upon: accompanying, connected with or immediately following as a consequence. Page 72.

attributes: qualities, features or characteristics belonging to or an inherent part of someone or something. Page 60.

attributing: of or related to the action of assigning a specific characteristic to (something). Page 206.

auditor: a practitioner of Scientology. The term comes from the Latin *audire,* "to listen." Hence, an auditor is one who listens; a listener. Scientology is employed by an auditor in Scientology *processing.* Processing is the verbal exercising of an individual in exact Scientology processes (exercises and drills) and is a unique but precise form of mental and spiritual counseling. Scientology processing helps place the individual in better control of himself, his mind, the people and the universe around him. The purpose of the auditor is to help increase the ability of the individual. Page 74.

authoritarian: of or relating to authoritarianism. Page 34.

authoritarianism: the system or practice of an *Authority,* one who is a supposed expert or one whose views and opinions on a subject are likely to be accepted without question and without reference to facts or results. Under authoritarianism individual freedom of judgment and action would be neglected in favor of absolute obedience to "experts." Page 40.

Authority: 1. a collection of experts or a supposed expert whose views and opinions on a subject are likely to be accepted without question and without reference to facts or results. Page 34.
2. the power to require and receive submission; the right to expect obedience; superiority. Page 38.

axiom(s): statements of natural laws on the order of those of the physical sciences. Page 25.

Babylon: the capital of *Babylonia*, an ancient empire of southwest Asia (located in the area now called Iraq) which flourished ca. 2100-689 B.C. The most important city in western Asia during this time period, Babylon was famous for its magnificent temples and palaces. Page 205.

bacteria: single-cell organisms, some of which cause disease. Page 26.

bad cause: things, actions, etc., that are very destructive. Page 175.

badlands: extensive areas of heavily eroded, uncultivatable land with little vegetation. Page 215.

barbarism: an absence of culture; uncivilized ignorance marked by wild, violent cruelty. Page 191.

bared: exposed to view; revealed. Page 129.

barriers: spaces, energy movements or obstacles. Page 100.

baser: lower in value, place, position, degree, scale or rank. Page 92.

basic personality: the individual himself. The basic individual is not a buried unknown or a different person, but an intensity of all that is best and most able in the person. Page 237.

batty: insane; crazy. Page 236.

behooves: is right and proper or appropriate for somebody; necessary for. Page 192.

being(s): a person; an identity. Page 60.

beingness: the condition of being is defined as the result of having assumed an identity. For example, one's own name, one's own profession, one's physical characteristics. Each or all of these things could be called one's beingness. Beingness is assumed by oneself, or given to oneself, or is attained. Page 261.

bell tolls, for whom the: a reference to a line from a religious essay by English poet John Donne (1572-1631), which reads in part: "No man is an island, entire of itself; every man is a piece of the continent, a part of the main...any man's death diminishes me, because I am involved in mankind; and therefore never send to know for whom the bell tolls; it tolls for thee." Historically, church bells have been tolled (rung slowly) to announce deaths. Page 61.

bent (upon): determined; set; resolved. Page 64.

besting: getting the better of, defeating, beating. Page 102.

bigoted: utterly intolerant of any creed, belief or opinion that differs from one's own. Page 274.

blighting: destroying the promise of; ruining or spoiling. Page 241.

bloodletter: a person who is warlike or eager for the shedding of blood. Page 159.

blunted: having the force or keenness weakened or impaired. Page 61.

born: brought into existence; created. Page 116.

borne: endured or tolerated. Page 114.

botch: a job that has been badly done; an unskilled piece of work; mess. Page 116.

brains and brawn: intelligence (brains) and strength (brawn, muscular strength). Page 164.

bread: food or any means of survival or support. Page 259.

breaking: crushing the emotional strength or spirit of (someone). Page 157.

breaks faith: violates one's promise or word; acts as a traitor. *Break* means to violate by disregarding or failing to observe (something); to fail to keep one's word or pledge. *Faith* means a verbal promise, vow or pledge; the duty of fulfilling an obligation. Page 241.

brickbat(s): a piece of brick used as a weapon. Used figuratively to mean remarks or comments which are highly critical and typically insulting. Page 272.

brigandage: the action of a bandit robbing travelers in mountains, forests or along roads, usually as a member of a roving band. Page 103.

brute: someone viewed as strong, tough or focused on the physical aspects of life. Page 8.

Buddhist: of or relating to *Buddhism,* the religion founded by Gautama Siddhartha Buddha (563-483? B.C.), Indian religious philosopher and teacher. Buddhism emphasizes physical and spiritual discipline as a means of liberation from the physical world. *Buddha* means one who has attained intellectual and ethical perfection by spiritual means. Page 173.

carping: characterized by frequent ill-natured, disgruntled faultfinding. Page 64.

cast adrift: set aside, discarded or rejected without direction or stability. Page 164.

cast of characters: literally, the actors of a play. Hence, persons who are part of an actual event or series of events. Page 192.

catcalls: loud shouts or cries made to express disapproval. Page 274.

causation: the power, influence or source by which something comes into existence, an action takes place or by which an effect is created. Page 195.

cause: to act in such a way that some specific thing happens as a result; to produce an effect; to be the emanation point or source point of an action. Page 173.

cause-point: the source from which something emanates (flows out, as from a source or origin); the point of impulse. Page 173.

cave (oneself) in: *cave in* is a US Western phrase for mental or physical collapse as like being at the bottom of a mine shaft when the supports collapsed and left the person under tons of debris. To *cave oneself in* means to cause oneself to experience mental and/or physical collapse to the extent that one cannot function causatively. Page 245.

censored: having had any part removed or changed so as to suppress or control it or keep it from others. Page 141.

censorious: marked by or given to an inclination to severely condemn moral errors, flaws, etc.; highly critical. Page 182.

censured: criticized severely or blamed, sometimes formally or officially. Page 209.

cessation: a temporary or complete stopping; discontinuance. Page 137.

chain of command: a series of executive positions or of officers and subordinates in order of authority especially with respect to the passing on of orders, responsibility, reports, or requests from higher to lower or lower to higher. Page 139.

Chaldea: the ancient name given to the lands at the head of the Persian Gulf, south of Babylon. The Chaldeans conquered Babylon in the 600s B.C., establishing the Chaldean Empire (ca. 625-539 B.C.). Chaldea expanded and became the center of the civilized world until conquered by the Persians in 539 B.C. Page 215.

chant: say something monotonously or repetitiously. Page 100.

charged: entrusted with a task as a duty or responsibility. Page 39.

charge, in (one's, his, etc.): under one's care, control and responsibility. Page 140.

chart, off the: so as to no longer appear on a map because of being completely destroyed. Page 74.

checks: restrains; holds in restraint or control. Page 161.

Christian Science: a religion founded in 1879 by Mary Baker Eddy (1821-1910) and based upon some of the teachings of Jesus. Christian Scientists view the Bible as the ultimate authority, believe God is wholly good and all-powerful, deny the reality of the material world, arguing that sin and illness are illusions to be overcome by the mind and thus rely on spiritual healing rather than medical help in fighting sickness. Page 173.

Christie: John Reginald Christie (1898-1953), English murderer. He was convicted and hung for the murder of his wife, but also confessed to the murder of five other women whose bodies were found in the walls and under the floorboards of his home. Page 192.

chronically: in a manner that lasts a long time or that is in a continuing state. Page 65.

chute, down the: into a state of failure or ruin, deterioration or collapse. A *chute* is a descent or decline and alludes to an incline or steeply sloped channel used to convey water, grain, coal, etc., into a wagon, truck or other receptacle at a lower level. Page 246.

circulations: numbers of copies of a publication that are sold or distributed to readers in a given period. Page 260.

clean hands: the state or condition of being free from deceit or falsehood; honesty. Page 247.

Clear: the *Clear* is a person who is not aberrated. He is rational in that he forms the best possible solutions he can on the data he has and from his viewpoint. This is achieved through *clearing,* releasing all the physical pain and painful emotion from the life of an individual. See *Dianetics: The Modern Science of Mental Health.* Page 48.

clique(s): a small and exclusive party or group of people associated for unworthy or selfish ends, such as to impose themselves as supreme authority in a particular field. Page 139.

cloistered: sheltered or secluded from the world. Page 273.

clutching: seizing with or as with the hands. Hence, gripping or holding tightly or firmly to something, such as a belief, idea, concept, etc. Page 120.

code(s) of conduct: any set of principles or rules of conduct. Page 165.

cog(s): the term *cog* can be used derogatorily to describe an individual worker (a cog) as carrying out minor, automatic actions as part of a larger, uncaring "machine." This view of the working man as nothing but a "laborer" controlled by larger forces was popularized by Karl Marx in the late 1800s. Marx viewed the worker not as a creative, living individual but as merely part of a mass or class of similar "laborers" tediously carrying out their tasks. A *cog* is literally part of a cogwheel, a wheel that has teeth (called cogs) of hardwood or metal made to insert between the teeth of another wheel so that they mesh. When one cogwheel is rotated, the other wheel is turned as well, thus transferring the motion to drive machinery. *See also* **Marx.** Page 130.

cold-blooded: without emotion or pity; deliberately cruel. Page 260.

come around: to cease being angry, hurt, etc., and return to a better mood. Page 165.

come to grief: suffer misfortune or ruin. Page 250.

commodity(ies): something tangible and real, likened to raw material or a primary agricultural product that can be bought and sold. Page 100.

common denominator: something common to or characteristic of a number of people, things, situations, etc.; shared characteristic. Page 91.

commotion: agitated and noisy activity, confusion or disturbance. Page 35.

communication: something which is sent and which is received. The intention to send and the intention to receive must both be present, in some degree, before an actual communication can take place. It is one of the three parts of A-R-C (affinity, reality and communication). Page 26.

communication lag: the length of time intervening between the posing of the question or origination of a statement and the exact moment that question or original statement is answered. *Lag* means to fail to maintain a desired pace or to keep up with something; fall or stay behind. Page 150.

communication line(s): the routes along which communications (particles, messages, etc.) travel from one person to another. Page 138.

companies: military units of eighty to two hundred soldiers commanded by a captain. Page 103.

complement: to bring to perfection or completion; supply what is lacking. Page 140.

composition: the way in which the whole of something is made, especially the manner in which its different parts are combined or related. From a Latin word which means placed together. Page 93.

concentric: having a common center, as circles one within another. Page 85.

condensed: more dense or compact; said of a compressed area or volume. Page 93.

confront: 1. to meet something face to face, especially an obstacle that must be overcome. Page 103.
2. face and experience (those things that are). Page 128.

consciousness: the state of being conscious; awareness of one's own existence, sensations, thoughts, surroundings. Page 65.

consideration(s): 1. an idea or opinion or thought. Page 47.
2. something that is or is to be kept in mind in making a decision, evaluation of facts, etc. Page 157.
3. careful thought or deliberation. Page 174.

consideration, taking into: taking into account; considering. Page 105.

constitute (oneself): establish or set oneself up in a particular way, as in order to hold a certain position, function or the like. Frequently used in reference to the mental constitution (makeup or composition) of a person. Page 140.

constrain: force or compel someone to do something. Page 161.

context: the words or passages of text that come before or after a particular word that help to explain or determine its full meaning; the general sense of a word or a clarification of it. Page 91.

contradistinction: differentiation between two things by identifying their contrasting qualities. Page 157.

contusions: bruises or injuries in which the skin is not broken. Page 26.

convalescences: gradual recoveries of health and strength after illness. Page 194.

counterposed: placed in opposition. Page 105.

court(s): bodies of people before whom judicial cases are heard, also, the places where they meet. Page 242.

covert(ly): concealed, hidden or disguised; not openly practiced or shown. Page 92.

covetous: having a strong desire to possess something, especially something that belongs to another person. Page 241.

cowed: timid and giving in or tending to give in to the demands or the authority of others; frightened with threats or violence into submission or obedience. Page 193.

cozy position: *cozy* means convenient or beneficial, usually as a result of dishonesty and suggests an opportunistic or conspiratorial intimacy. A *cozy position* is a relationship between two or more parties that is beneficial, usually monetarily or for power, usually as a result of dishonesty, mutual opportunity, conspiracy, etc., as in "a cozy position between lobbyists and politicians." Page 34.

creditable: worthy of belief. Page 10.

credo: a strongly held belief or set of principles adopted as a guide to action or achievement. Page 136.

creed(s): any system or set of (religious) beliefs or of opinions. Page 160.

criteria: standards of judgment; rules or principles for evaluating or testing something; principles or standards by which something or someone may be judged or decided. Page 205.

criterion: a standard of judgment; a rule or principle for evaluating or testing something. Page 64.

crystal ball: a ball of clear crystal or glass, traditionally used by fortunetellers in predicting the future. Page 150.

culmination: the condition or state of having ended or arrived at a final stage or of having resulted in, often with the sense of having reached a most intense or decisive moment in the development or resolution of something. Page 25.

cult(s): an exclusive or closed (one which is not open or in communication with others) group of people who share some common interest or belief. Page 262.

culture: a group of microorganisms grown in a special substance under controlled conditions, as for scientific, medical or commercial purposes. Page 39.

cunning: knowledge of how to do a thing; skill in performance. Page 58.

currents: course of events; constant or frequent change of forces. Page 114.

curse: a cause of unhappiness or harm; a great evil. Page 100.

cycle-of-action: the sequence that an action goes through, wherein the action is started, is continued for as long as is required and then is completed as planned. Page 194.

daily bread: that by which one earns his or her living or day-to-day existence; means of survival; livelihood. *Daily bread* is the food or provisions necessary for day-to-day survival. Page 259.

dark operation(s): unethical or illegal business or activity, especially that of an *operator*, a shrewd individual who maneuvers people and events by blackmail and other illegal means for his own purposes. *Dark* means evil, wicked, unjust, secret and hidden. Also known as *black operations*. Page 229.

data: plural of *datum*. Page 33.

datum: a single piece of information, as a fact; something known or assumed. Page 36.

da Vinci, Leonardo: (1452–1519) Italian painter, draftsman, sculptor, architect and engineer who left notebooks with engineering and scientific observations that were in some cases centuries ahead of their time. Page 35.

decree, by: by formally declaring in an official order or ruling. Page 36.

defeatist: advocating or accepting defeat; describing a person who surrenders easily or who no longer resists defeat because of the conviction that further effort is futile (incapable of producing any result). Page 73.

degradation: a way of life without dignity, health or any social comforts; a condition of extreme poverty and uncaring neglect. Page 241.

demented: crazy; insane; mad. Page 182.

demise: death; the end of a person's existence. Page 26.

depression: 1. any period marked by slackening of business activity, increased unemployment, falling prices and wages, etc. Page 113.
2. a feeling of sadness in which a person feels there is no hope for the future. Page 272.

deranged: disturbed the order or arrangement of; upset the normal condition or function of. Page 113.

derive: obtain something from a source; form or develop out of something else. Page 8.

dermatitis: inflammation of the skin resulting in redness, swelling, itching or other symptoms. Page 73.

descend: to move from a higher to a lower place; come or go down. Page 94.

desolation: a feeling of loneliness, abandonment, sorrow, hopelessness and despair. Page 274.

desperate: facing the worst with firmness of mind or purpose; making a final, ultimate effort; giving all. Page 130.

detached eye: *detached* in this sense means unaffected by emotional involvement or any form of bias. *Eye* here means a point of view or way of thinking. Hence, a *detached eye* is a point of view that is impartial or free from involvement. Page 99.

determinism: power of choice or decision. Page 26.

Dianetics: Dianetics is a forerunner and substudy of Scientology. Dianetics means "through the mind" or "through the soul" (from Greek *dia,* through and *nous,* mind or soul). It is a system of coordinated axioms which resolve problems concerning human behavior and psychosomatic illnesses. It combines a workable technique and a thoroughly validated method for increasing sanity, by erasing unwanted sensations and unpleasant emotions. See entry for *Dianetics: The Modern Science of Mental Health* and other Dianetics books in the Further Study in the Appendix. Page 273.

Dickens: Charles Dickens (1812-1870), popular English author who wrote about nineteenth-century society and whose stories often depicted eccentric characters. *See also* **"waiting for something to turn up."** Page 115.

differentiate(tion): to see, notice or find out the difference between two or more things. Page 204.

Dillinger: John Dillinger (1902-1934), an infamous American bank robber, murderer and two-time prison escapee who was declared "public enemy number one" in 1933 for his role in numerous bank robberies and murders, including that of a police officer, performed by himself and members of a gang he organized. Page 192.

diminish(ed): make smaller or less in scope, quality, etc. Page 62.

discharged: relieved charge (a store or accumulation of force or energy) from; unburden. Page 74.

discipline(s): the practice of penalizing or punishing people in order to train them to obey rules or a code of behavior. Page 183.

discount: to underestimate the significance or effectiveness of; minimize or set aside as irrelevant. Page 47.

discourses: verbal interchanges of ideas; conversations. Page 94.

dispensable: able to be replaced or done without. Page 129.

diverting: drawing off to a different course, purpose, etc. Page 150.

docile: easily managed or handled. Page 160.

doctrine: something that is taught or laid down as true concerning a particular subject or department of knowledge. Page 116.

doggone: an exclamation used to express irritation, anger, disgust, etc. Page 8.

doomed: condemned to suffer a dreadful fate, especially one that is inescapable. Page 101.

dope: drugs to induce a state of extreme excitement and happiness or to satisfy an addiction; illegal drugs. Page 242.

downhill: into a worse or inferior condition. Page 174.

down pat: mastered or learned perfectly. Page 118.

downscale: located at or moving toward the middle or lower end of a scale; to a lower or worse condition, state or position. Page 150.

drafted: chosen or taken for required military service by drawing from a group. Page 106.

dream up: to invent. Page 260.

driven: forced someone or something into a particular state or condition, often an extremely negative one. Page 193.

driving: compelling or forcing to work, often excessively. Page 128.

ducks: lowers quickly, especially so as to avoid something, such as in lowering the head in a fight to avoid a punch from one's opponent. Used figuratively. Page 114.

Durant, Will: William (Will) James Durant (1885-1981), American author, historian and popularizer of philosophy. Durant's book *The Story of Philosophy* (1926) explains in simple language the central ideas of the world's greatest philosophers and tells of their lives. Despite criticism from many critics and scholars who condemned the book for its simplified style, easily comprehensible to the average reader, *The Story of Philosophy* was immensely popular, selling millions of copies in a dozen languages. Page 271.

duress: pressure, such as force or threats, to make somebody act or think in a certain way against their will or better judgment. Page 191.

dwelling upon: spending time upon or lingering over (a thing) in action or thought; remaining with the attention fixed on. Page 104.

dwindling spiral: the worse an individual or situation gets, the more capacity he or it has to get worse. *Spiral* refers to a progressive downward movement, marking a relentlessly deteriorating state of affairs, and considered to take the form of a spiral. The term comes from aviation where it is used to describe the phenomenon of a plane descending and spiraling in smaller and smaller circles, as in an accident or feat of expert flying, which if not handled can result in loss of control and a crash. Page 104.

economy: 1. careful avoidance of financial waste. Page 113.
2. efficient use of resources. Page 140.

effect(s): something produced by an action or a cause; result; consequence. Page 73.

effect-point: that to which something emanates (flows out, as from a source or origin); the receipt-point of an impulse. Page 173.

Egypt: in ancient times a flourishing kingdom and one of the earliest known civilizations, located in northeast Africa, primarily in the region along the length of the Nile River. Page 205.

elaborate: marked by intricate and often excessive detail; complicated. Page 261.

electrons: negatively charged particles that form a part of all atoms. Page 57.

element(s): 1. a component or constituent of a whole. Page 57.
2. groups of people singled out within a larger group by identifiable behavior patterns, common interests, etc. Page 259.

emanated: caused; originated; sent forth. Page 175.

embellished: had extra details or information added, especially ones that are not true. Page 193.

embrace: to take up readily or gladly and willingly believe in and seek to further, defend and support. Page 86.

embroiled: involved in conflicts and problems. Page 251.

eminent: high in station, rank or repute; prominent; distinguished. Page 34.

empire, win: to expand and obtain increased influence, command and control. Page 141.

Energy: a potential of motion or power. It would be a force or flow or the potential force or flow from something to something; or the ability to accomplish work; or the ability to make motion or movement. It is potential or actual motion or force. Page 85.

enigma: something hard to understand or explain. Page 48.

ensue: to follow as a consequence. Page 9.

enterprise: any systematic purposeful activity or type of activity, especially that which is undertaken with an economic or commercial end in view. Page 196.

entities, survival (non-survival): *entities* are things that have independent or separate existence; things that have distinctness of character and being. *Entities* refer to persons who are the source of something, in this case, survival or non-survival. Page 162.

enturbulate: to cause to be turbulent, agitated and disturbed. Page 137.

enturbulence: a turbulent, agitated or disturbed state; commotion and upset. Page 64.

envision(ed): imagine (something not yet in existence); picture in the mind, especially some future event or events. Page 121.

eons: an immeasurably or indefinitely long period of time. Page 245.

equilateral: all sides the same. Page 93.

eradicate(ing): remove or get rid of someone or something completely. Page 73.

err: to be mistaken or incorrect. Page 35.

esoteric: beyond the understanding or knowledge of most people; intended for or understood only by a few. Page 19.

essence, in (the final): (most) basically or fundamentally. Page 12.

ethic(s): rationality toward the highest level of survival for the individual, the future race, the group, Mankind and the other dynamics taken up collectively. Ethics are reason. Man's greatest weapon is his reason. Page 135.

euthanasia: also called "mercy killing," the act of putting to death painlessly or allowing to die, as by withholding extreme medical measures, a person or animal suffering from an incurable, especially a painful, disease or condition. Page 64.

evaluated: considered or examined in order to judge its significance, worth or quality; assessed. Page 36.

evaluation: the act of considering or examining something in order to judge its significance, worth or quality. Page 36.

evil tidings: news or information (tidings) that is destructive, damaging or harmful. Page 193.

ex-barbers: a *barber* is one who cuts hair and shaves or trims men's beards. *Ex-barbers* is a reference to modern medical practitioners (physicians, psychologists and psychiatrists), who descended from barbers that, over the centuries, carried out crude surgery and dentistry. Psychology was heavily influenced by Russian physiologist

Ivan Petrovich Pavlov (1849-1936), who conducted behavior experiments with dogs. Pavlov presented food to a dog while he sounded a bell. After repeating this procedure several times, the dog (in anticipation) would salivate at the sound of the bell, whether or not food was presented. Pavlov concluded that all learning, even the higher mental activity of Man, depended on such a process and his experiments are the basis of "behavioral psychology" today. Page 158.

expeditiousness: the quality or state of being *expeditious,* acting or done with speed and efficiency. Page 136.

expends: uses or spends a lot of time, energy, care, etc., in order to do something. Page 164.

experience: the process or fact of personally observing, encountering or undergoing something; confronting something. Page 63.

exterior: situated outside. Page 99.

extort: to obtain something, such as money or information, from someone by using force, threats or other unfair or illegal methods. Page 260.

face of, in the: when confronted with. Page 182.

facile: able to act, work or proceed easily and smoothly. Page 37.

faith: 1. a religion or a system of religious beliefs. Page 25.
2. confidence or trust in a person or thing. Page 141.

faith, breaks: violates one's promise or word; acts as a traitor. *Break* means to violate by disregarding or failing to observe (something); to fail to keep one's word or pledge. *Faith* means a verbal promise, vow or pledge; the duty of fulfilling an obligation. Page 241.

fallacy: a false or mistaken idea; error. Page 160.

fascist: one who practices *fascism,* a governmental system led by a dictator having complete power, which forcibly suppresses opposition and criticism and regiments all industry, commerce, etc. Page 63.

fate: something (unfavorable) that inevitably happens to somebody or something. Page 113.

fatten: become rich. Page 260.

FBI: abbreviation for *Federal Bureau of Investigation,* a United States government agency established to investigate violations of federal laws and to safeguard national security. Page 196.

feat: an act or accomplishment showing unusual skill, imagination, etc. Page 129.

fiction(s): 1. a story describing imaginary events and people, that is written, performed or told with the intention of entertaining an audience. Page 35.

2. something invented or imagined; a made-up story. Page 261.

fiddle: to play with (using the fingers) as if in an aimless way. Page 118.

fight shy: keep away from; avoid. Page 162.

fixation: a preoccupation with one subject, issue, etc.; obsession. Page 195.

flash(es): a sudden or brief manifestation or occurrence, from the literal meaning of *flash*, a sudden, quick outburst or issuing forth of flame or light. Page 205.

flight of fancy: an idea or thought that is very imaginative; creative thinking. *Flight* here means passing above and beyond ordinary bounds. *Fancy* is the mental faculty through which visions and fantasies are imagined; an invention created by the mind. Page 36.

flint ax: an ancient tool or weapon formed by shaping a piece of *flint*, a hard gray rock that chips into pieces with sharp cutting edges. Page 35.

Floyd, Pretty Boy: Charles Arthur Floyd (1904-1934), American gangster, bank robber and killer, who robbed more than thirty banks, murdering at least ten men, half of whom were police officers. Page 192.

fluke(s): an accidental advantage or result of an action; chance happening. Page 127.

flung: thrown, especially with great violence or force. Used figuratively. Page 118.

foes: opponents or enemies of somebody or something. Page 114.

folded up: broke down; collapsed; failed. Page 236.

foolhardy: showing boldness or courage but not wisdom or good sense. Page 72.

forbidding: unfriendly or threatening in appearance. Page 273.

forebears: ancestors; forefathers. Page 12.

foregone conclusion: a decision or opinion formed in advance of proper consideration or full evidence. Page 41.

formidable: difficult to deal with; requiring great skill to overcome; challenging. Page 118.

fortune: 1. a supposed power thought of as bringing good or bad to people; chance, regarded as affecting human activities. Page 127. 2. great financial wealth or material possessions. Page 128.

for whom the bell tolls: a reference to a line from a religious essay by English poet John Donne (1572-1631), which reads in part: "No man is an island, entire of itself; every man is a piece of the continent, a part of the main...any man's death diminishes me, because I am involved in mankind; and therefore never send to know for whom the bell tolls; it tolls for thee." Historically, church bells have been tolled (rung slowly) to announce deaths. Page 61.

founded: laid the base of or supported, such as a conclusion, with evidence or reasoning. From Latin *fundus* "bottom, base." Page 114.

fragility: the quality of being easily broken or liable to be damaged or destroyed. Page 158.

free rein: unrestricted freedom of movement, choice or action. A *rein* is a long narrow strap of leather attached to a bit on either side of a horse or other animal's head, by which it is controlled and guided by the rider or driver. The term *free rein* derives from the literal meaning of using reins to control a horse. Page 191.

French Revolution: a revolt in France from 1789 to 1799 which overthrew the royal family and the aristocratic class and system of privileges they enjoyed. The revolution was in part a protest against France's absolute monarchy, entrenched and unproductive nobility and the consequent lack of freedom for the middle classes. During the revolution, 300,000 people were arrested and 17,000 were beheaded under the guillotine. Page 103.

fruits: the benefits or advantages of an activity. Page 242.

Galen: full name, Claudius Galenus (A.D. 130?-200), Greek physician who wrongly believed that the liver converted food into blood which then flowed into the rest of the body and was absorbed. His undisputed authority in medicine discouraged original research and inhibited medical progress until the sixteenth century when British physician William Harvey (1578-1657) discovered that blood circulated throughout the body and was propelled to the heart, thus proving wrong Galen's theories. Page 34.

game: in Scientology, a *game* consists of freedom, barriers and purposes. Page 83.

get into (things): to become occupied with, interested, involved or absorbed in (something). Page 106.

get out of (things): to avoid, escape or get away from. Page 106.

gives: yields or furnishes as a product, consequence or effect. Page 49.

gnostic: of or relating to knowledge. Page 25.

goal(s): a known objective toward which an action is directed with the purpose of achieving that end. Page 3.

golden rule(s): a rule of ethical conduct. The golden rule is traditionally phrased: "Do unto others as you would have them do unto you." Page 173.

good old days: an expression used when referring to a former time, remembered with nostalgia, as being better than the present, and sometimes despite modern improvements in science, technology, etc. Page 7.

grace: elegance or beauty of form, manner, motion or action. Page 8.

greatest good, on the basis of the: a reference to the optimum solution to any problem: that solution which brings the greatest benefits to the greatest number of dynamics. Such solutions lead to increased survival on the majority of the dynamics. Page 208.

grimly: in a manner that is firm and determined. Page 122.

grind: something that is routine, dull and tedious, such as work. Page 114.

gritting one's teeth: summoning up one's strength to face unpleasantness or overcome a difficulty. *Grit* is used here in the sense of both clamping one's teeth together and grinding them with effort. Page 115.

grounded, well: thoroughly familiar with the essential details or data of a subject; having good training in or much knowledge of a subject. Page 261.

guise: outward appearance or form of someone or something. Page 102.

gulf: a gap that serves as a means of separation; a wide interval. Page 139.

habitable: suitable or good enough to live in. Page 9.

half-murder: punish severely or be very angry with. Page 158.

half-wit: one who does not have all his mental abilities or intelligence; a stupid or senseless person. Page 159.

halls of learning: buildings used by a college or university for teaching or research. Page 271.

hand in hand: in the manner of things that are inseparably interrelated; in union. Page 238.

harbinger: a person who announces or signals the approach of something. Page 193.

hard luck: misfortune; bad luck. Used to show one thinks someone has brought the misfortune on himself. Page 159.

Harvey: William Harvey (1578-1657), English physician who, by using scientific procedures and experimentation, discovered the circulation of the blood and the role of the heart, thus proving wrong the theories of Galen. Page 34.

hasten: speed up, accelerate. Page 63.

heavy weather: a figurative phrase meaning troubles, obstacles, difficulties, etc., that arise. Literally *heavy* here means overcast and dark skies, perhaps with rain, gloomy clouds, etc. It can also refer to the turbulence, great force or intensity of high waves at sea that may make the normal operations on a ship very difficult. Thus, if one is facing trouble, obstacles, difficulties, etc., he could figuratively be said to be in "heavy weather." Page 274.

hence: therefore; as a result. Page 61.

hitherto: up to this time; until now. Page 65.

Hitler: Adolf Hitler (1889-1945), German political leader of the twentieth century who dreamed of creating a master race that would rule for a thousand years as the third German Empire. Taking over rule of Germany by force in 1933 as a dictator, he began World War II (1939-1945), subjecting much of Europe to his domination and murdering millions of Jews and others considered "inferior." He committed suicide in 1945 when Germany's defeat was imminent. Page 64.

hodgepodge: a confused mixture; mess. Page 175.

honor: adherence to actions or principles considered right, moral and of high standard; integrity; a fine sense of what is right and wrong. Page 19.

host: a large number; a great quantity. Page 25.

humanities: branches of learning (or, *humanity,* a branch of learning) concerned with human thought and relations, especially philosophy, literature, history, art, languages, etc., as distinguished from the natural sciences (sciences such as biology, chemistry and physics that deal with phenomena observable in nature); the social sciences including sociology (the science or study of the origin, development, organization and functioning of human society), psychology, economics, political science, etc. Originally, the *humanities* referred to education that would enable a person to freely think and judge for himself, as opposed to a narrow study of technical skills. Page 39.

humanity: the quality of being humane; kindness; benevolence. Page 273.

hung up: halted or snagged in something. Page 175.

ideology: the doctrines, opinions or way of thinking of an individual, class, etc.; specifically, the body of ideas on which a particular political, economic or social system is based. Page 48.

illusion(s): a false idea; belief or opinion (about oneself, another, a situation, etc.) that does not agree with facts or reality. Page 165.

imbecilic: characteristic of someone with a very low intelligence. Page 160.

imparting: making something known; telling; relating. Page 193.

impenetrable: incapable of being understood. Page 271.

incapacitating: depriving of ability or strength; making incapable or unfit; disabling. Page 237.

incidence: the rate of occurrence of something, especially of something unwanted. Page 105.

incumbent upon: resting upon as a duty or obligation. Page 135.

index(es): an indicator, sign or measure of something. Page 205.

indispensable: essential, that cannot be gotten rid of or done away with. Page 129.

individuality: the sum of the characteristics or qualities that sets one person apart from others; individual character. Page 84.

indoctrinated: instructed in a principle, subject, etc. Page 173.

indoctrination: the action of giving instructions especially in the basics of a subject. Page 27.

industrialist: one owning or engaged in the management of an especially large-scale industry. Page 114.

industry: economic activity concerned with the processing of raw materials and manufacture of goods in factories. Page 129.

inexplicably: in a way that cannot be explained, understood or accounted for. Page 113.

infanticide: the practice of killing newborn babies. Page 236.

infects: taints or contaminates with something that affects quality, character or condition unfavorably; corrupts or affects morally. Page 228.

infinity: unlimited extent of time, space or quantity; unlimited capacity, energy, excellence or knowledge. Page 38.

initiative: the power, ability or readiness to begin or to follow through energetically with a plan or task. Page 101.

inkblots: a reference to *inkblot tests,* any of several psychological tests in which varied patterns formed by blotted ink on paper are shown to and interpreted by the subject (person), his reactions being analyzed and used as a supposed guide to his personality. Originally developed by Swiss psychiatrist Hermann Rorschach (1884-1922). Page 150.

inner circle: a small group of people within a larger group, who have a lot of power, influence and special information. Page 272.

Inquisition: a special court established in the late 1400s under the rulers of Spain, Queen Isabella I (1451-1504) and King Ferdinand V (1452-1516). The Spanish Inquisition identified, interrogated with torture to extract "confessions," imprisoned, tried in court and punished by burning at the stake persons of Jewish, Muslim and later, Protestant faiths who had beliefs contrary to the Roman Catholic Church. As ordered by Tomás de Torquemada (1420-1498), the first and most notorious grand inquisitor and also the personal priest of the Spanish king and queen, thousands were driven from Spain and thousands more were killed. The Inquisition was finally abandoned by Spain in 1834. Page 204.

insidiously: having a gradual, cumulative and usually hidden destructive effect. Page 251.

insofar as: to such an extent, to such a degree. Page 136.

inspiration: a stimulation or animating external influence on the mind (and emotions) that prompts one (creatively) to think a certain way, take action, etc. Used here humorously. Page 121.

intellect: capacity for thinking and acquiring knowledge, especially of a high or complex order; mental capacity. Page 149.

intellectual: a person who spends his time in study or who claims to belong to a group of highly intelligent people. Page 271.

interminably: in a way that is annoyingly continuous or unceasing; endlessly. Page 36.

in that: for the reason that. Page 25.

in the face of: when confronted with. Page 182.

invalidate: to weaken or make valueless; discredit, nullify. Page 117.

invalidation: refuting, degrading, discrediting or denying something someone else considers to be fact; criticizing, discrediting or destroying the validity of someone or their thoughts, emotions or efforts. Page 193.

invoke: quote, rely on or use something such as a law in support of an argument or case. Page 228.

iron steed: a reference to a motorcycle. A *steed* is a horse, especially a high-spirited one. Page 8.

Jesuit: a member of the *Jesuits,* a Roman Catholic religious order (Society of Jesus) founded in 1534. Mainly a missionary order, the Jesuits used education as the primary means of spreading their beliefs. Page 157.

Job: in the Old Testament, a man whose faith was tested, with God's permission, by Satan. Job was prosperous and happy, faithfully praising God. Attempting to make Job curse God, Satan destroyed all that Job owned, killed his children, burned his sheep and belongings, stole his camels, slaughtered his servants, blew down his house, and finally, struck Job with sores from head to foot. False friends urged Job to abandon his beliefs and curse God. But even in misery, Job would not curse God and remained faithful. The story culminates in a dramatic conversation between Job and God, and due to Job's steadfast faith, God restores his health and provides him with twice as much as he had before. Page 174.

junior: subordinate to; smaller in scale to something larger or more powerful. The use is military in origin and refers to an individual of lower position or rank. Page 102.

keel: the long piece of wood or steel along the bottom of a boat that forms the major part of its structure and helps to keep the boat balanced in the water. Page 149.

keynotes: the prime underlying elements or themes (of something). Page 229.

keystone: a supporting principle; the chief element in a system; that upon which the remainder rests or depends. A *keystone* is the stone of an arch (typically the uppermost stone), which being the last put in, is regarded as keying or locking the whole structure together. Page 91.

large, at: as a whole; in general. Page 228.

learned: showing or characterized by deep or extensive knowledge; well-informed. Page 34.

least, to say the: used as an understatement (implying the reality is more extreme, usually worse). Page 236.

leeway: degree of freedom of action or permitted discretion; room for choice; extra time, space, materials or the like, within which to operate. Page 159.

length, at: after a time; finally. Page 228.

Lenin: Vladimir Ilyich Lenin (1870–1924), Russian leader of the communist revolution of 1917 who, through force and terror, then became dictator of the USSR (Union of Soviet Socialist Republics, a former group of Russian controlled states) from 1917 to 1924. Page 217.

license: abusive disregard for what is considered right, proper, etc.; excessive liberty. Page 243.

licked: defeated as in a fight, game or contest. Page 160.

light of, in the: taking into account; considering. Page 139.

loosely: not strictly; broadly. Page 102.

loosely, speak: talk in a manner that is not exact or precise. Page 260.

luxury: the unusual intellectual or emotional pleasure or comfort derived from some specified thing. Page 196.

machine age: a name given to an era notable for its extensive use of mechanical devices. Used in reference to the twentieth century because of its widespread use of machines and automation. Page 228.

magic hand, wave(s) a: a variation of *wave a magic wand,* used figuratively to mean produce wonderful appearances or results in one's environment, like the magical effects thought of as produced by a magician and coming from supernatural causes. A *magic wand* is literally a small, thin stick used in performing magic. Page 8.

main, in the: for the most part; mainly. Page 127.

malfunction: the action or fact of functioning badly or imperfectly, or of failing to operate in the normal or usual manner. Page 26.

Man: the human race or species, humankind, Mankind. Page 11.

man: 1. an adult male person, as distinguished from a woman or boy. Page 8.

2. a human being, without regard to sex or age; a person. Page 38.

manifestation: a visible demonstration or display of the existence, presence, qualities or nature of something. Page 41.

man in the street: the ordinary person, especially someone without specialized knowledge of the field in question. Page 271.

manner of the day: the current way or method in which something is done or happens. Page 197.

marbles: small hard balls, usually of glass, used in children's games. Used humorously in reference to its figurative meaning of common sense or sanity, as in the phrase *to lose one's marbles*, which means to go insane. Page 150.

margin: an amount over and above what is strictly necessary, included, for example, for safety reasons or to allow for mistakes, delays or other unforeseen circumstances. Page 114.

markedly: in a manner that is noticeable or to a significant extent. Page 72.

marry, up and: to marry someone without warning. *Up* in the phrase *up and marry* means to carry out abruptly and surprisingly. Page 149.

Martians: supposed inhabitants of the planet Mars. Page 196.

martyr: someone who willingly suffers death rather than give up his religion. Page 173.

Marx: Karl Marx (1818-1883), German political philosopher whose works formed the basis of twentieth-century communism and who viewed society as a conflict between the capitalists (factory owners) and the workers. Marx and his fellow communists accused the capitalists of miserable working conditions such as poorly paying the workers, of long hours under unhealthy and dangerous conditions and of abusive child labor.

mass(es): compounded, compressed energy particles; matter. Page 101.

materiality: material things; that which is material (formed or consisting of matter; physical); the physical world rather than the mind or spirit. Page 273.

mathematics: the branch of science concerned with number, quantity and space and applied to physics, engineering and other subjects. Page 25.

maxim: a concisely expressed principle or rule of conduct, or a statement of a general truth. Page 105.

measuring stick: something against which one measures or judges value, worth, condition, etc. A *measuring stick* is an instrument, as a graduated rod, having a sequence of marks at regular intervals, which is used as a reference in determining length, height, etc. Used figuratively. Page 34.

mechanical arts: arts, trades and occupations concerned with machines or tools or with the design and construction of machines or tools. Page 207.

mechanics: the procedural or operational details (*of* something). When applied to theories, specifically, *mechanics* means the explanation of phenomena by the assumption of mechanical action; the explanation of how something works. Page 33.

mechanism: the agency or means by which an effect is produced or a purpose is accomplished, likened to the structure or system of parts in a mechanical device for carrying out some function or doing something. Page 10.

medico: a physician or surgeon; doctor. Page 260.

menace: a threat of danger, harm, injury, etc. Page 63.

men of God: holy or devout persons devoted to the service of God, as saints or prophets. Page 48.

Merchants of Chaos: people who make a profession out of relaying, supplying or forwarding bad news, confusion and chaos. *Merchants* are people who buy and sell commodities for a profit. By extension, they are persons noted for, or who have a particular interest in, some specific activity, or who make a profession of it. *Merchant* is often used with a qualifying word, sometimes derogatorily. Page 259.

merger: the combining of two things into one. Page 48.

mid-flight: in the middle of a course of action or established pattern. Page 161.

militarist: somebody who zealously supports and promotes military ideals. Page 260.

millennia: thousands of years. Plural form of *millennium,* a period of one thousand years. Page 48.

mis-emotion: *mis-* abbreviation of miserable, misery. *Mis-emotion* is anything that is unpleasant emotion such as antagonism, anger, fear, grief, apathy or a death feeling. Page 175.

mis-selection: a mistaken, wrong or incorrect selecting. *Mis-* means mistaken, wrong, incorrect; thus *mis-selection* means an instance of selecting (choosing of one person or thing in preference to another), that is *mistaken,* based on an incorrect understanding or perception. Page 149.

mission: a special task or purpose that a person or group believes it is their duty to carry out; a duty or function given to or assumed by a person or group. Page 27.

monocell: an organism composed of a single cell. Page 58.

monopoly: the exclusive possession or control of something. Page 275.

moral code: an agreed-upon code of right and wrong conduct. It is that series of agreements to which a person has subscribed to guarantee the survival of a group. The origin of a moral code comes about when it is discovered through actual experience that some act is more non-survival than pro-survival. The prohibition of this act then enters into the customs of the people and may eventually become a law. Page 243.

mud, product of the: a reference to a theory that Man arose from mud. This theory alleges that chemicals formed in mud and through certain combinations and accidental patterns, a primitive single cell was formed. This primitive cell then collided with other such cells and through further accident formed a more complex structure of single cells which made itself into a unit organism. From this combination of cells, Man was supposedly eventually formed. Page 3.

muffled: kept down, suppressed. Page 48.

muffs: coverings for the hands that differ from gloves in that they do not have divisions for fingers (also known as *mittens*). Muffs that are securely fastened can be used as a restraint. Page 160.

myriad: an indefinitely great number; innumerable. Page 137.

Napoleon: Napoleon Bonaparte (1769-1821), French military leader. He rose to power in France by military force, declared himself emperor and conducted campaigns of conquest across Europe until his final defeat by armies allied against him in 1815. Half a million men died in the Napoleonic Wars (1799-1815). Page 192.

navigating: planning, recording and controlling the course and position of (a ship or an aircraft). Hence, following a planned course on, across or through. Page 113.

nebulously: in a manner that is hazy, vague, indistinct or confused. Page 34.

ne plus ultra: the ultimate; especially the finest, best, most perfect. Page 159.

neurosis: an emotional state containing conflicts and emotional data inhibiting the abilities or welfare of the individual. Page 105.

nobility: high ideals or excellent moral character and behavior. Page 19.

noble: characterized as being unselfish and morally good; having or showing admirable qualities. Page 182.

nobles: people who are born into a high class who have special social or political status in a country. Page 103.

no-game condition(s): a condition that occurs when one wins completely or loses utterly. When a person continues to play a game after a totality of win or lose, it is removed from his reality of game because he can no longer really respond while doing it. For example, someone has a game with an automobile of trying to get away at the traffic lights first. After the fifth accident, it is a no-game condition because he still has to drive but knows he has lost the game and it is no longer a game for him. Page 100.

non-communication: no communication; inability to communicate. Page 149.

non-survival: from *non,* implying negation or absence of and *survival.* Hence, *non-survival* is a negation or absence of survival, the act of remaining alive, of continuing to exist, of being alive. Page 60.

nuclear physics: the branch of physics that deals with the behavior, structure and component parts of the center of an atom (called the nucleus), which constitutes almost all of the mass of the atom. Also in reference to the atom bomb created by nuclear physicists. Page 48.

nullify: reduce to nothing, counteract completely the force, effectiveness or value of. Page 73.

objective: independent of what is personal or private in one's thoughts and feelings; not dependent on the mind for existence, as opposed to subjective. Page 38.

observe(d): to regard with attention, especially so as to see or learn something. Page 19.

obsessive cause: a reference to a state or condition characterized by only causing things, thus resembling an *obsession,* the domination of one's thoughts or feelings by a persistent idea, image, desire, etc. Page 173.

occasioned: brought about; caused. Page 26.

oil crisis: a shortage of oil occurring in the United States and certain European countries beginning in the early 1970s. The shortage was caused mainly by restrictions placed on oil trade by the Organization of Petroleum Exporting Countries (OPEC), which regulated the amount of oil produced by its member countries and set the prices for its export. The restrictions were intended to punish the United States and some of its allies for supporting Israel in its 1973 conflict with the Arab states. The situation caused widespread panic, severe shortages of gasoline and extremely inflated prices. The crisis continued at varying levels through the 1970s and by 1980 oil prices were ten times those of 1973. Page 240.

old saw: an old saying, often repeated. Page 105.

on the way out: going down in status or condition; dying. Page 236.

open mind: a mind accessible to all arguments or points of view. Page 19.

optic nerve(s): the nerve that carries signals from the eye to the brain. *Optic* means of or relating to the eye or vision. Page 274.

optimum: most favorable or desirable; best. Page 62.

orders of, on the: in particular ways, like; after the fashion of. Page 140.

organism: an individual form of life; a body. Page 27.

out-ethics: an action or situation in which an individual is involved, or something the individual does, which is contrary to the ideals, best interests and survival of his dynamics. Page 236.

outline: a general description covering the main points of something, such as a subject. Page 102.

outmoded: not acceptable by present standards; obsolete. Page 63.

outward bound: departing this life, dying, or preparing, starting or going in the direction of death. From the nautical use meaning headed in an outward direction, as toward foreign ports; going away from home. Hence, *"outward bound toward death."* Page 62.

overburden: a weight or load, as of information, data, etc., that is excessive, more than someone can easily assimilate, retain or use; an overload. Page 37.

overtly: in a way that is open to view or knowledge; plainly or readily apparent. Page 195.

palpable: easily perceptible by the mind or one of the senses, as to be almost able to be felt physically. *Palpable* comes from the Latin meaning "that can be touched." Page 100.

Pan-determinism: *pan* means *across* and *determinism* means the ability to determine the course of or the decision about. Hence, *Pan-determinism* means the willingness of an individual to determine the action of self and others. It means wider determinism than self.

An individual who is Pan-determined is determined across the eight dynamics. Page 102.

panorama: a complete and comprehensive view or range. Page 99.

parity: the state or condition of being equal, or on a level with as in amount, status or character. Page 149.

part and parcel: an indivisible element in something. Page 241.

particles: (small) pieces of something; parts, portions or divisions of a whole. Page 92.

particular: an individual fact or item. Page 117.

pastime: a specific form of amusement (as a recreation, game or sport). From the French term *passe-temps* meaning pass time. Page 99.

pat, down: mastered or learned perfectly. Page 118.

pawn: something that can be used for one's advantage. Page 12.

peddle: sell something illegal, especially drugs. Page 242.

pennyweights: units of weight equal to ¹/₂₀th of an ounce or 1.6 grams. The pennyweight was once the weight of a silver penny. Page 74.

pension: a sum of money paid regularly as a retirement benefit for past services to an employer. Page 113.

perpetrated: committed or performed. Page 191.

person of, in the: in the physical form of. Page 150.

pervert: 1. turn from the proper use, purpose or meaning; misapply or misdirect. Page 141.

2. a person with abnormal sexual behavior. Page 241.

phenomena: the plural of *phenomenon*, a fact, occurrence or circumstance observed or observable. Page 218.

philosophy: 1. the love, study or pursuit of wisdom, or of knowledge of things and their causes, whether theoretical or practical; the study of the truths or principles underlying all knowledge, being (reality) or conduct. From Greek *philos,* loving and *sophia,* learning. Page 25.

2. a set of opinions, ideas or principles; a basic theory; a view or outlook, as those belonging to a particular field as in political philosophy. Page 115.

physical sciences: any of the sciences, such as physics and chemistry, that study and analyze the nature and properties of energy and nonliving matter. Page 26.

physical universe: the universe of matter, energy, space and time. The universe of the planets, their rocks, rivers and oceans, the universe of stars and galaxies, the universe of burning suns and time. Page 12.

pilots: tests of something, for example a proposed program or process, used to discover and solve problems before full implementation. Page 140.

plankton: a collection of small microscopic organisms, including algae, that float or drift in great numbers in fresh or salt water at or near the surface and serve as food for fish and other larger organisms. Page 39.

plant: a building or group of buildings for the manufacture of a product; a factory. Also the equipment, including machinery, tools, instruments and fixtures, and the buildings containing them, necessary for an industrial or manufacturing operation. Page 114.

plea: an earnest and urgent request. Page 37.

plot: to lay out or show some process, condition or course of something, as if with the precision used to chart the course of a ship, draw a map of an area, etc. Page 102.

plotting: arranging something beforehand (sometimes in a secret way). Page 106.

plutonium: a radioactive metallic element that is used in nuclear reactors and nuclear weapons. Page 74.

political slavery: deprivation of political freedom, a state of being enslaved or completely dominated. Page 229.

polo: a game played on horseback by two teams of four players each, who attempt to drive a small wooden ball through the opponents' goal. Page 99.

populace: the common people of a nation as distinguished from the higher classes. Page 103.

pose: put forward or present something such as a problem, a danger or the like. Page 38.

poses: puts forth for examination; questions. Page 60.

postulate(d): assume (something) to be true, real or necessary, especially as a basis for reasoning. Page 35.

postulate(s): an assumption, especially as a basis for reasoning. Page 160.

potent: influential; strong; powerful. Page 115.

power of choice: the ability or capacity to determine or decide something (such as a course of action). Page 106.

practice license: to engage in abusive disregard for what is considered right, proper, etc.; to take excessive liberty. Page 243.

predecessor(s): something previously in use or existence that has been replaced or succeeded by something else. Page 25.

predetermined: given a direction or tendency toward a particular course of action beforehand. Page 26.

predisposition: a condition which makes one inclined or liable to disease, illness, etc. Page 26.

preponderance: the fact or quality of being greater in influence, force, weight, etc.; prevailing (having superior power or influence). Page 34.

prerogatives: rights, privileges, etc., limited to a specific person or to persons of a particular category. Page 136.

Pretty Boy Floyd: Charles Arthur Floyd (1904-1934), American gangster, bank robber and killer, who robbed more than thirty banks, murdering at least ten men, half of whom were police officers. Page 192.

Prime Datum: a supposed datum (piece of information, fact, etc.) that is fundamental or basic and from which other data may derive or proceed. Page 36.

privates: soldiers of the lowest rank. Page 103.

process(es): 1. an exact series of steps, actions, drills and exercises utilized in Scientology processing to help place the individual in better control of himself, his mind, the people and the universe around him. Page 25.

2. gives *processing*. Page 27.

processing: Scientology counseling. By processing is meant the verbal exercising of an individual utilizing exact Scientology processes to help place the individual in better control of himself, his mind, the people and the universe around him. Page 105.

prophet(s): inspired teachers; those who speak for God or any deity as interpreters of his will. Page 174.

proscribe: prohibit something that is considered undesirable. Page 138.

pro-survival: from *pro,* in favor of, and *survival*. Hence, *pro-survival* is something in favor of or in support of survival, the act of remaining alive, of continuing to exist, of being alive. Page 243.

protons: the positively charged particles that form a part of all atoms. Page 57.

province: sphere or field of activity or authority. Page 26.

provocation: something that makes someone angry or irritated especially when done deliberately. Page 183.

psychology: modern psychology, developed in 1879 by German professor Wilhelm Wundt (1832-1920) at Leipzig University in Germany, who conceived that Man was an animal without a soul and based all of his work on the principle that there was no psyche (a Greek word meaning spirit). Psychology, the study of the spirit (or mind) then came into the peculiar position of being a study of the spirit which denied the spirit. Page 11.

psychosis: a conflict of commands which *seriously reduce* the individual's ability to solve his problems in his environment, to a point where he cannot adjust himself to some vital phase of his environmental needs. Page 149.

psychosomatic: *psycho* refers to mind and *somatic* refers to body; the term *psychosomatic* means the mind making the body ill or illnesses which have been created physically within the body by the mind. The description of the cause and source of psychosomatic ills is contained in *Dianetics: The Modern Science of Mental Health*. Page 26.

purpose(s): intended or desired result; aim; goal. Page 41.

quandary: a state of uncertainty. Page 209.

quarters: a living space; a place of residence. Page 159.

quenched: subdued or destroyed; overcome. Page 165.

quicksand: a bed of soft or loose sand saturated with water and having considerable depth, yielding under weight and therefore tending to suck down any object resting on its surface. Used figuratively. Page 40.

rabble-rousers: people who stir up hatred, violence or other strong feelings in a group or a crowd through emotionalism, especially for political reasons. Page 114.

race: a group of persons related by common history, nationality, geographic distribution or physical characteristics (color, facial features, size, etc.). Page 84.

races (win at the): organized contests run over a regular course, such as horse racing or dog racing, where people bet money on a potential winner with the hope of attaining money. Page 115.

ratio: the corresponding relationship between two or more things; proportional relation. A *ratio* is sometimes expressed as a number or amount in relationship to another number or amount. For example, if a person spends ten hours inside and one hour outside, the ratio is 10:1 or ten to one. Page 33.

rationale: the reasoning or principle that underlies or explains a particular course of action, or a statement setting out these reasons or principles. Page 135.

rave: to utter as if in madness. Page 182.

reactively: irrationally; in a manner that shows one is affected by the reactive mind. Page 244.

reactive mind: that portion of a person's mind which works on a totally stimulus-response basis (given a certain stimulus it gives a certain response), which is not under his volitional control, and which exerts force and the power of command over his awareness, purposes, thoughts, body and actions.

reality: "that which appears to be." Reality is fundamentally agreement. What we agree to be real is real. It is one of the three parts of A-R-C (affinity, reality and communication). Page 38.

realize: make real; give reality to. Page 62.

realm: an area or field of activity, thought, study or interest. Page 26.

rear guard: the rear portion of an advancing army or armed force. Hence, any group of people who, rather than lead, trail far behind others in new developments, ideas or actions. Page 48.

recompense: payment given to someone in exchange for doing work or performing a service. Page 260.

recourse to: the act or instance of turning to something for aid, use or help. Page 26.

recriminations: accusations made against someone who has brought previous accusations. Page 219.

reflexive: directed back on itself; of or concerning something that bends or turns backwards, such as an action that is directed back upon the origination point. Page 173.

regime: a form of government or rule; political system. Also, a system, especially one imposed by a government. Page 113.

render: to make, to cause to be or become of a certain nature, quality, etc. Page 209.

reprehensibly: in a manner deserving strong disapproval or criticism. Page 240.

resorts: goes to or falls back on someone or something in time of need; turns to for aid or relief. Page 115.

resurgences: acts of rising again or springing again into being or vigor. Page 63.

revenue: money that comes into a business from the sale of goods or services. Page 260.

revolutionary: of or having to do with *revolution,* the overthrow and replacement of an established government or political system, usually by the people governed. Page 100.

revolutionary forces: that group of people who supported and fought in the Russian Revolution of 1917. The revolutionary forces, led by the Communists under Vladimir Lenin (1870-1924), overthrew the czar (emperor of Russia) and established a Communist government. Page 217.

rheumatism: disorder of the extremities (limbs, hands or feet) or back, characterized by pain and stiffness. Page 73.

rock: source of danger or destruction, suggestive of a shipwreck. Page 149.

rocks, on the: in or into a state of disaster or ruin. Page 150.

romantic novels: novels representing heroic or marvelous deeds, romantic exploits, usually in a historical or imaginary setting. Page 241.

Rome: a reference to the empire of ancient Rome (which at its peak included western and southern Europe, Britain, North Africa and the lands of the eastern Mediterranean Sea) that lasted from 27 B.C. to A.D. 476, when it fell to invading Germanic tribes. In the last century of the Empire, conditions began a steady decline due to economic disintegration, weak emperors, invading tribes and the central government providing few services and little protection while demanding more taxes. Page 205.

rompers: a one-piece garment for a child combining a shirt and short pants. Page 162.

root: the source or origin of a thing. Page 149.

rows: noisy disputes or quarrels. Page 151.

Royal Medical Academy: a reference to the *Royal College of Physicians of London*, the oldest medical institution in England, established in 1518. Page 35.

ruling passion: a chief or predominating object of intense interest in a particular subject or activity. Page 236.

rumormonger: one who spreads false or damaging reports concerning the character or reputation of others. *Monger* literally means one who trades or sells something. Page 193.

sacrificing: letting go; firing or demoting. Page 140.

sages: very wise men, especially persons who are widely respected for their wisdom, experience and judgment. Page 174.

sake: interest or benefit. Page 100.

sanity: rationality. A man is sane in the ratio that he can compute accurately, limited only by information and viewpoint. Page 34.

saw: an old saying, often repeated. Page 105.

scatheless: unharmed or unhurt. Page 183.

school of thought: a way of thinking about something, as by a group of people who share the same attitude or opinion. Page 41.

science: knowledge; comprehension or understanding of facts or principles, classified and made available in work, life or the search for truth. A science is a connected body of demonstrated truths or observed facts systematically organized and bound together under general laws. It includes trustworthy methods for the discovery of new truth within its domain and denotes the application of scientific methods in fields of study previously considered open only to theories based on subjective, historical or undemonstrable, abstract criteria. The word *science*, applied to Scientology, is used in this sense – the most fundamental meaning and tradition of the word – and not in the sense of the *physical* or *material* sciences. Page 25.

sciences, (physical): any of the sciences, such as physics and chemistry, that study and analyze the nature and properties of energy and nonliving matter. Page 26.

scientific: of or pertaining to science or the sciences; using or practicing the methods of scientists or devised by scientists. Page 27.

Scientologist: one who betters the conditions of himself and the conditions of others by using Scientology technology. Page 25.

Scientology: Scientology addresses the spirit. Scientology is used to increase spiritual freedom, intelligence, ability and produce immortality. It is further defined as the study and handling of the spirit in relationship to itself, universes and other life. Page 3.

scrapheap: a place for dumping old, useless things. Page 271.

sedatives: drugs that are primarily used to induce drowsiness and sleep. Sedatives are habit-forming and can cause severe addiction problems. Page 248.

self-determined: having self-determinism. Page 102.

self-determinism: a condition of determining the actions of self. Self-determinism is a First Dynamic determinism. That is, "I can determine my own actions." Page 102.

senior: superior; of greater influence; on a higher level than (something). The use is military in origin and refers to an individual holding a position of higher rank. Page 102.

sequitur: something that sequentially follows another thing or a conclusion that logically follows something already stated or mentioned. From Latin *sequitur*, it follows. Page 150.

service record: the record of a person's employment in a branch of military service. For example, a naval service record contains documents such as birth certificate, school certificates, letters of commendation, enlistment contract, history of assignments, performance record, medical record, rank, etc. Page 274.

set: to establish for others to follow; furnish as a pattern or model. Page 129.

setting forth: presenting or declaring something; laying something out. Page 84.

Shakespeare: William Shakespeare (1564–1616), English poet and author of many plays; the most famous playwright of all time. Page 35.

sheerest: completely; without qualification. Page 129.

shepherded: guarded or watched over carefully as a shepherd does with sheep. Page 162.

shortcomings: faults or failures to meet a certain standard, typically in a person's character or conduct. Page 86.

shun: keep away from (something or someone); avoid deliberately. Page 104.

shy away: draw back or avoid. Page 128.

Sicily: largest island in the Mediterranean, Sicily is a region of Italy, located off the southwestern tip of the mainland. Page 215.

slant: a point of view. *Title.*

slashed: cut one's way using sweeping strokes with or as if with a sharp instrument. Used figuratively. Page 129.

slave master: one who dominates or controls others, likened to someone who owns other persons who have no freedom or personal rights. Page 273.

smallpox: a serious infectious disease that caused spots which left deep marks on the skin and was often fatal. Smallpox has been eradicated worldwide by vaccination (treatment which makes one immune to a disease) programs. Page 196.

social: pertaining to, devoted to or characterized by friendly companionship or relations; seeking or enjoying the companionship of others; friendly; sociable. Page 162.

social animal: someone living, or inclined to live, in communities; someone desirous of enjoying the society or companionship of others. Used derogatorily. Page 160.

solidities: things which are solid, firm or hard. Page 92.

solvent: something which solves or settles; something which has the power to cause to disappear or vanish such things as problems, situations or the like. Page 93.

sorrow: mental and emotional suffering caused by loss or disappointment; sadness, grief or regret. Page 74.

Space: viewpoint of dimension. There is no space without viewpoint. There is no space without points to view. Page 85.

spark (something) off: to stimulate or initiate (interest, activity, spirit, etc.). Page 217.

species: a group or class of animals or plants having certain common and permanent characteristics which clearly distinguish it from other groups and which can breed with one another. Also used figuratively. Page 158.

spiral, dwindling (downward): the worse an individual or situation gets, the more capacity he or it has to get worse. *Spiral* refers to a progressive downward movement, marking a relentlessly deteriorating state of affairs, and considered to take the form of a spiral. The term comes from aviation where it is used to describe the phenomenon of a plane descending and spiraling in smaller and smaller circles, as in an accident or feat of expert flying, which if not handled can result in loss of control and a crash. Page 75.

square blocks: a reference to the cubes (square blocks) used in psychological tests in which a person does certain requested actions with the blocks (usually colored) to supposedly test his mental state. Page 150.

stable: 1. firmly established; solid; fixed. *Stable* derives from Latin *stabilis* meaning firm, steadfast. Page 116.

2. (of a person) having a consistently steady, dependable character. Page 157.

stalked: walked angrily and stiffly. Page 121.

stand up to: to meet or deal with; to confront or face up to. Page 116.

stations: positions people hold in society or in an organization in terms of social standing or rank. Page 205.

steadied: made firmer in position or place; made freer from change or variation. Page 118.

stem: arise or originate from, or be caused by something or someone. Page 182.

stepped forward: presented oneself, as if by taking a single step, and entered into an activity or situation to set about doing something. Page 121.

stick, makes them: causes (something) to persist or remain active or effective. Page 260.

storm: a disturbance in the air above the Earth, involving strong winds and usually rain (sometimes with lightning and thunder), snow, sleet or hail. Hence, any (violent) disturbance or upheaval in political, social or domestic affairs. Page 114.

Story of Philosophy, The: the title of a book, published in 1926, by American author, historian and popularizer of philosophy Will Durant (1885–1981). The book explains in simple language the central ideas of the world's greatest philosophers and tells of their lives. Despite criticism from many critics and scholars who condemned the book for its simplified style, easily comprehensible to the average reader, *The Story of Philosophy* was immensely popular, selling millions of copies in a dozen languages. Page 272.

strained: of personal relations, a situation, etc., subjected to a dangerous degree of tension, forced to a point of threatened disharmony. Page 251.

straitjacket: a garment made of strong material and designed to bind the arms and restrict a person's movements. A *straitjacket* is used to keep a violently disoriented person from harming themselves or others. Page 160.

stress: suppression on one or more parts of one's life. Page 71.

strive: to exert oneself vigorously; try hard. Page 60.

strut: to walk with a vain, pompous bearing, as with head erect and chest thrown out, as if expecting to impress observers. Page 182.

studiously: with considerable attention; deliberately. Page 128.

subjective: existing in the mind; dependent on the mind or on an individual's perception for its existence as opposed to objective. Page 38.

subordinate: to make subject, subservient or dependent. Page 228.

subversive: someone involved in activities intended to undermine or overthrow an authority. Page 165.

succeedingly: coming next in order; subsequently. Page 93.

successively: in succession, following one upon another. Page 85.

succumb: fail to survive; cease to exist. Page 58.

superstition(s): unreasoning awe or irrational fear of what is unknown or mysterious, especially in connection with religion; religious beliefs or practices founded upon fear or ignorance. Page 12.

suppress(ed): to squash, to sit on, to make smaller, to refuse to let reach, to make uncertain about his reaching, to render or lessen in any way possible by any means possible to the harm of the individual and for the fancied protection of the suppressor. Page 64.

survival (non-survival) entities: *entities* are things that have independent or separate existence; things that have distinctness of character and being. *Entities* refer to persons who are the source of something, in this case, survival or non-survival. Page 162.

suspect: regarded with suspicion or distrust. Page 73.

swallowed: took in so as to envelop or enclose. Page 48.

swan song: last act or manifestation of someone or something before dying, from the belief that the dying swan sings. Page 205.

sweeping: wide in range or effect; general. Page 71.

swing through it: a reference to the motion of a boxer hitting or punching with a swinging motion of the arm(s). Hence, to battle one's way through something conceived of as threatening or attacking. Page 114.

switchboard: the central part of a telephone system used by a company where telephone calls are answered and connected (switched) to the appropriate person or department. Page 116.

synthetic: not real or genuine; artificial. Page 106.

taking sides: giving one's support to one person or group in contrast to that of an opposing one; being partial to one side. Page 103.

Tao: the *Tao Teh King,* the doctrine and philosophy written by Lao-tzu (604–531 B.C.) in verse form. It literally means "The Way" and is the foundation of *Taoism,* a Chinese philosophy that advocates a simple life and a policy of noninterference with the natural course of things. Page 25.

target end: the person at the receiving end, from *target,* the person, object or place selected as the aim of an attack. Page 175.

taxidermist: one who practices the art or skill of preparing, stuffing and presenting dead animals for exhibition in a lifelike state. Page 40.

technique(s): the specialized procedures and methods used in any specific field. Page 33.

technology: a method or methodology that applies technical knowledge; the application of scientific knowledge for practical purposes. Page 138.

technology: the methods of application of an art or science as opposed to mere knowledge of the science or art itself. In Scientology, the term *technology* refers to the methods of application of Scientology principles to improve the functions of the mind and rehabilitate the potentials of the spirit, developed by L. Ron Hubbard. Page 227.

techno-space society: a society which has advanced to the point of space travel and is technologically oriented. *Techno-* means technology. Page 228.

teeth, gritting one's: summoning up one's strength to face unpleasantness or overcome a difficulty. *Grit* is used here in the sense of both clamping one's teeth together and grinding them with effort. Page 115.

tenement: a run-down and often overcrowded apartment house. Page 238.

tenets: principles, doctrines or beliefs held as a truth. Page 36.

therapeutic: having a good effect on the body or mind; contributing to a sense of well-being. Page 26.

therapy: a curative power or quality. Page 157.

thwart: block or obstruct, as to prevent someone's plans from succeeding. Page 204.

tide: a body of flowing water; a current. Used figuratively here in the *"tide of life"* to mean the moving force of life. Page 63.

"tides" of the blood: a reference to earlier theories of the blood, such as those of Greek physician Galen (A.D. 130?–200), who wrongly believed that the liver converted food into blood which then flowed into the rest of the body and was absorbed. *Tide* refers to something like the tides of the sea (which rise and fall every twelve hours), as in experiencing an increase followed by a decrease or a rising and then a falling. Page 35.

tidings: news or information. Page 193.

Time: any time you say time, you're just saying persist. That is the motto of time. That is what time is, that is what time means. Time means a uniform rate of persistence. Page 85.

tinsel path: *tinsel* is a thread, strip of paper, plastic or metal used to produce a sparkling or glittery effect. Used figuratively to mean something marked by a deceptively brilliant or valuable appearance. Hence a *tinsel path* would be an attractive course of action or conduct with little real worth or value. Page 114.

tolerance: the ability to allow an action, situation or the like to occur without feeling any discomfort or uneasiness. Page 106.

tomes: books, especially very heavy, large or learned books. Page 160.

tone(s): one's emotional level. Page 92.

Tone Scale: a scale of emotional tones which shows the levels of human behavior. These tones, ranged from the highest to the lowest, are in part Serenity, Enthusiasm, Conservatism, Boredom, Antagonism, Anger, Covert Hostility, Fear, Grief and Apathy. Page 92.

tradition: a belief, custom or way of doing something that has existed for a long time among a particular group of people or a set of these beliefs or customs. Page 25.

trained Scientologist: someone with special knowledge in the handling of life. He achieves this through *training,* which is a formal activity (differing from casual reading or interest) imparting the philosophy or technology of Scientology to an individual or group and culminates in the award of a grade or certificate. Page 27.

tranquilizer(s): any of certain drugs given as a supposed calming agent in controlling various emotional conditions. Page 248.

trap(s): a contrivance (as a mechanical device that springs shut suddenly) used for catching game or animals. Used figuratively. Page 101.

travail: pain or suffering resulting from conditions which are mentally or physically difficult to overcome. Page 99.

treacherous: giving a false appearance of safety or reliability; untrustworthy or insecure. Page 149.

tricky: difficult to deal with or handle and requiring skill, caution or tact (skill or sensitivity to what is correct in dealing with others, so that one does not upset or annoy them). Page 149.

true-blue: unwaveringly loyal or faithful. Page 121.

turbulence: the quality or state of being turbulent (characterized by or showing disturbance, disorder or violence); violent disorder or commotion. Page 37.

turns loose: lets go, releases. Page 115.

typhoid: a serious and sometimes fatal bacterial infection of the digestive system, caused by contaminated water or food. Page 39.

undermine: to weaken or cause to collapse by removing underlying support, as by digging away or eroding the foundation. Used figuratively. Page 37.

unerring: always right or accurate. Page 138.

unto: a formal way of saying *to*, showing that something is given to someone. Page 173.

unwittingly: unknowingly; without awareness. Page 237.

up and marry: to marry someone without warning. *Up* in the phrase *up and marry* means to carry out abruptly and surprisingly. Page 149.

urges: drives, impulses. Page 83.

validation: official confirmation or approval of, as persons, procedures, etc. Page 38.

vantage point: a position or location that provides a broad view or perspective of something. Page 99.

Veda, the: the *Vedic Hymns,* the earliest recorded learned writings. They are the most ancient sacred literature of the Hindus (the natives of India) comprising over a hundred books still in existence. They tell about evolution, about Man coming into this universe and the curve of life, which is birth, growth, degeneration and decay. Page 25.

villainy: evil conduct; extreme wickedness. Page 242.

visionaries: dreamers; people whose ideas, plans, etc., are impractical or too fantastic. Page 100.

vital: 1. full of vigor; energetic. Page 59.

2. extremely important and necessary to the survival or continuing effectiveness of something. Page 127.

vitality: enthusiastic physical strength or mental vigor. Page 65.

vivisection: the practice of operating on living animals to study structures, function and disease. Page 35.

volition: the act of willing, choosing or resolving; the exercise of one's will. Page 194.

voodoo: a body of beliefs and practices originally from Africa that includes magic and the supposed exercise of supernatural powers through the aid of evil spirits. Page 74.

wage earner: a person who works for wages; a person whose earnings support a family household. Page 149.

"waiting for something to turn up": a reference to a philosophy of life displayed by the character Mr. Wilkins Micawber, from the well-known nineteenth-century novel *David Copperfield,* by English author Charles Dickens (1812-1870). Micawber, a friend of Copperfield's, comes up with many ideas to bring about wealth, and although his attempts fail, he never gives up and remains certain something will "turn up." Page 115.

wake, in (one's): *wake* is the visible trail (of agitated and disturbed water) left by something, such as a ship, moving through water. Hence, a condition left behind someone or something that has passed; following as a consequence. Page 119.

wanting: lacking or absent. Page 99.

war cry: literally a cry or shout of troops in battle. Figuratively it is something shouted to encourage or rally a group. Page 103.

warped: mentally twisted; turned away from truth or fact or from a healthy, sane condition. Page 203.

wealth of, to the: a coined phrase meaning to the general good, welfare, well-being of, etc. Page 140.

weed out: to separate out or remove something undesirable or unwanted. Page 196.

weight felt, make his: a variation of *to throw one's weight around,* to effectively assert oneself or one's authority. Used figuratively. Page 159.

welfare state: a political system in which a government assumes the primary burden for its citizens, such as by paying them directly when out of work or financially supporting their health needs. Page 137.

Western culture: of or pertaining to the culture of the countries and people of Europe and the Americas. Page 150.

whereas: while on the contrary; in comparison with the fact that. Page 84.

win empire: to expand and obtain increased influence, command and control. Page 141.

wise, in this: in this way or in this manner. Page 103.

witch hunts: investigations carried out, supposedly to uncover and expose disloyalty, dishonesty or the like, usually based on doubtful or irrelevant evidence. From the witch hunts of Salem, Massachusetts, in 1692, which led to the execution of twenty people, based on little evidence, for allegedly practicing witchcraft. Page 203.

wither away: to lose the freshness of youth, as from age. Page 3.

withhold: to keep from doing or saying something; to keep in check or under restraint; to hold back, restrain. Page 174.

word of mouth: communication using the spoken word, as distinguished from writing or other methods of expression. Page 262.

wrong target: an incorrect selection of an objective to attempt or attack. Page 194.

yardstick: a standard used to judge the quality, value or success of something. Page 243.

yearns: wants something very much, often with a feeling of frustration because of the difficulty or impossibility of fulfilling the desire. Page 101.

year of our Lord: a particular year since the originally given date of the birth of Jesus Christ, December 25 A.D. 1. (*A.D.* is Latin for *Anno Domini* which means "in the year of our Lord.") Page 165.

yesteryear: the past, often a period with a set of values or a way of life that no longer exists. Page 129.

Index

A

aberration

    accident-prone child and, 165

    evil and, 161

    possible to eradicate, 73

    subjects of ethics and justice and, 245

ability

    to handle confusion, 118

    to hold a job, 127

abortion, 236

accidents

    accident-prone, 63

        child and, 165

    of fate, 113

    spiritual malfunction and, 26

    why people cause themselves, 237

actions (acts)

    too many harmful, 237

adult

    rights around children, 157

    treating, as child is treated, 158

affinity, 91-94

    communication and, 94

        relationship to reality and, 93

    definition, 91

    manager having, for group, 140

Affinity, Reality and Communication, *see* **A-R-C**

agreement(s)

    communication and basis for, 94

    organisms and, 62

    public test for sanity and, 34

    reality and, 93

alcohol addiction, 250

Anger, 92

Animal Dynamic

    definition, 85

answers

    Scientology and basic truth of, 261

Antagonism, 92

Anti-Social Personality, 191-197

    artist, magnet for, 195

    attributes, 192-195

347

fights

Third Party and, 216

First Dynamic, 86

dead and most wrong on, 239

definition, 84

man stealing from employer and, 247

unhappiness on, 251

force

control with, 62

physical universe, capable only of, 58

foreman

bad control by, 119

bringing order, 117

emergencies and confusion of, 116

"forgiveness"

greatness versus, 182

Fourth Dynamic

definition, 84

freedom

barriers and, 100

element of a game, 100

for child and you, 162

for honest men, 227

"freedom from," 101

knowledge and, 273

must be deserved, 227

Social Personality having, 204

total, 101

truth shall set you free, 272

unhappiness and, 104

way to, 275

French Revolution, 103

fundamentals, 40-41

of Scientology, 37

student discovering, 34

future generations, 61

G

Galen, 34

games

ability to play, 106, 129

definition, 99

dynamics and, 102

forced to play, 106

freedom, barriers and purposes, 103

life and, 99-106

Pan-determinism and, 102

Self-determinism and, 102

three elements of, 105

generalities

speaking in broad, 193

goal maker

goals as envisioned by, 139

goals

correcting failure to recognize, 137

envisioned by goal maker, 139

games and, 105

groups and, 135

H

ingredients of successful, 128

one must be able to control, 127

play and reason for hard, 165

stable datum of society, 128

worker

importance of, 130

world

age five versus thirty, looking at, 8

handling confusions of workaday, 113-122

kept going, by a handful of desperate men, 130

living in a very fast-paced, 11

worth

individual, 139

wrongness

people specializing in, 209

right and, 237-241

Y

you

subject matter of Scientology, 3

young

"I can get and hold a job," 120, 122

Z

zero

influence, 246

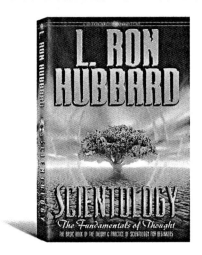